LOST RAILWAYS OF ESSEX

Robin Jones

COUNTRYSIDE BOOKS

NEWBURY, BERKSHIRE

First published 2008
© Robin Jones Diamond Head 2008

COUNTRYSIDE BOOKS
3 Catherine Road
Newbury, Berkshire

To view our complete range of books,
please visit us at
www.countrysidebooks.co.uk

ISBN 978 1 84674 111 1

The cover picture of a 2MT Class Mogul loco, with a local train,
leaving Glemsford station is from an original painting
by Colin Dogget

Produced through MRM Associates Ltd., Reading
Typeset by Jean Cussons Typesetting, Diss, Norfolk
Printed by Cambridge University Press

*All material for the manufacture of this book
was sourced from sustainable forests*

CONTENTS

ACKNOWLEDGEMENTS

Special thanks to the following for their help in compiling this book: the Great Eastern Railway Society, the Gresley Society, Lens of Sutton Association, Jenny Jones, Ross Jones, Keith and Sheila Lobley, Brian Morrison, Bevan Price, Andrew Neale, Malcolm Root, Geoff Silcock, Mangapps Railway Museum, 53A Models of Hull Collection.

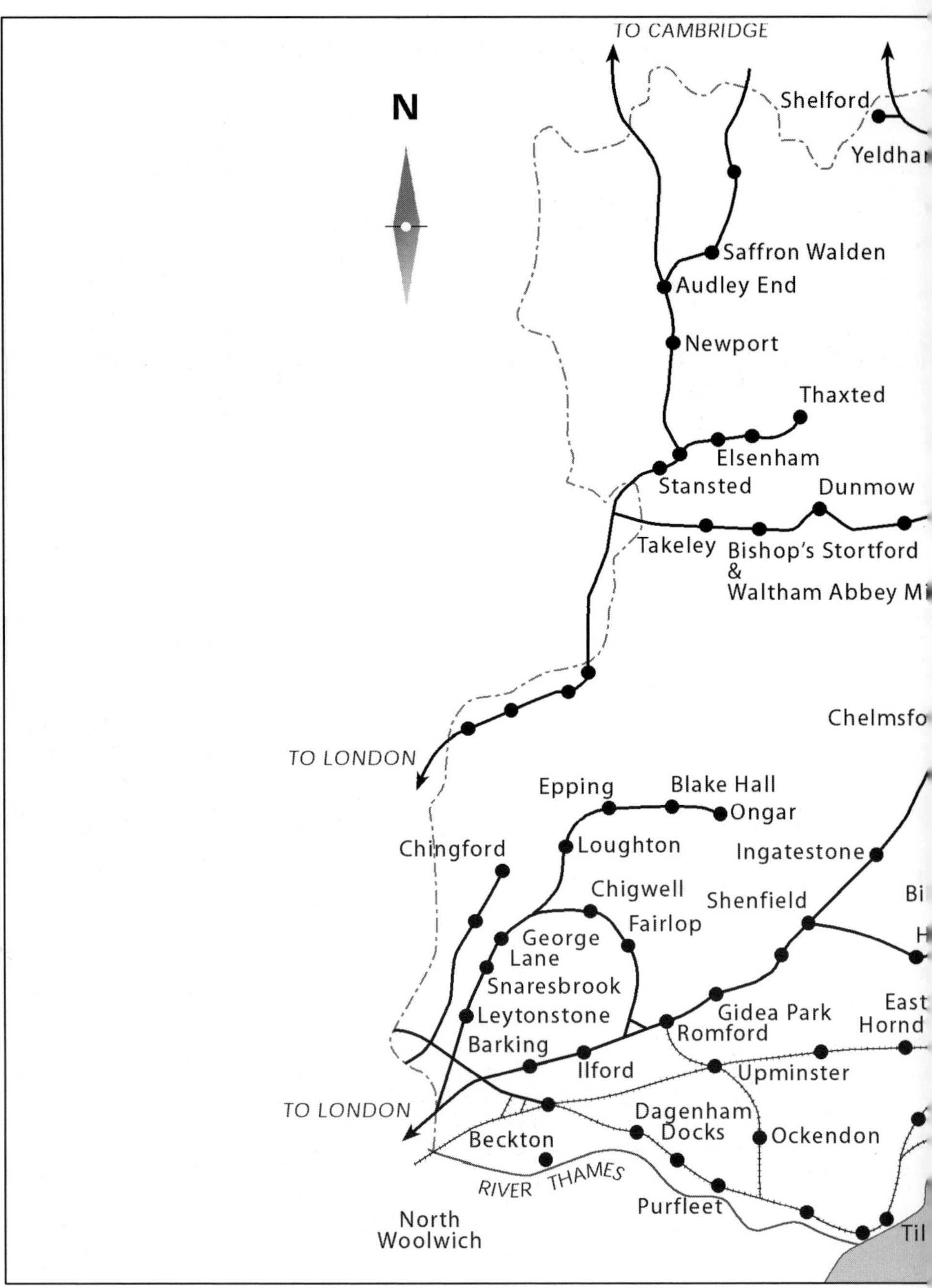

N
TO CAMBRIDGE
Shelford
Yeldha
Saffron Walden
Audley End
Newport
Thaxted
Elsenham
Stansted
Dunmow
Takeley
Bishop's Stortford
&
Waltham Abbey M
Chelmsfo
TO LONDON
Epping
Blake Hall
Ongar
Chingford
Loughton
Ingatestone
Chigwell
Shenfield
Bi
Fairlop
George
Lane
H
Snaresbrook
East
Leytonstone
Gidea Park
Hornd
Barking
Romford
Ilford
Upminster
TO LONDON
Dagenham
Beckton
Docks
Ockendon
RIVER THAMES
Purfleet
North
Woolwich
Til

ESSEX RAILWAYS c.1950 *(Not to Scale)*

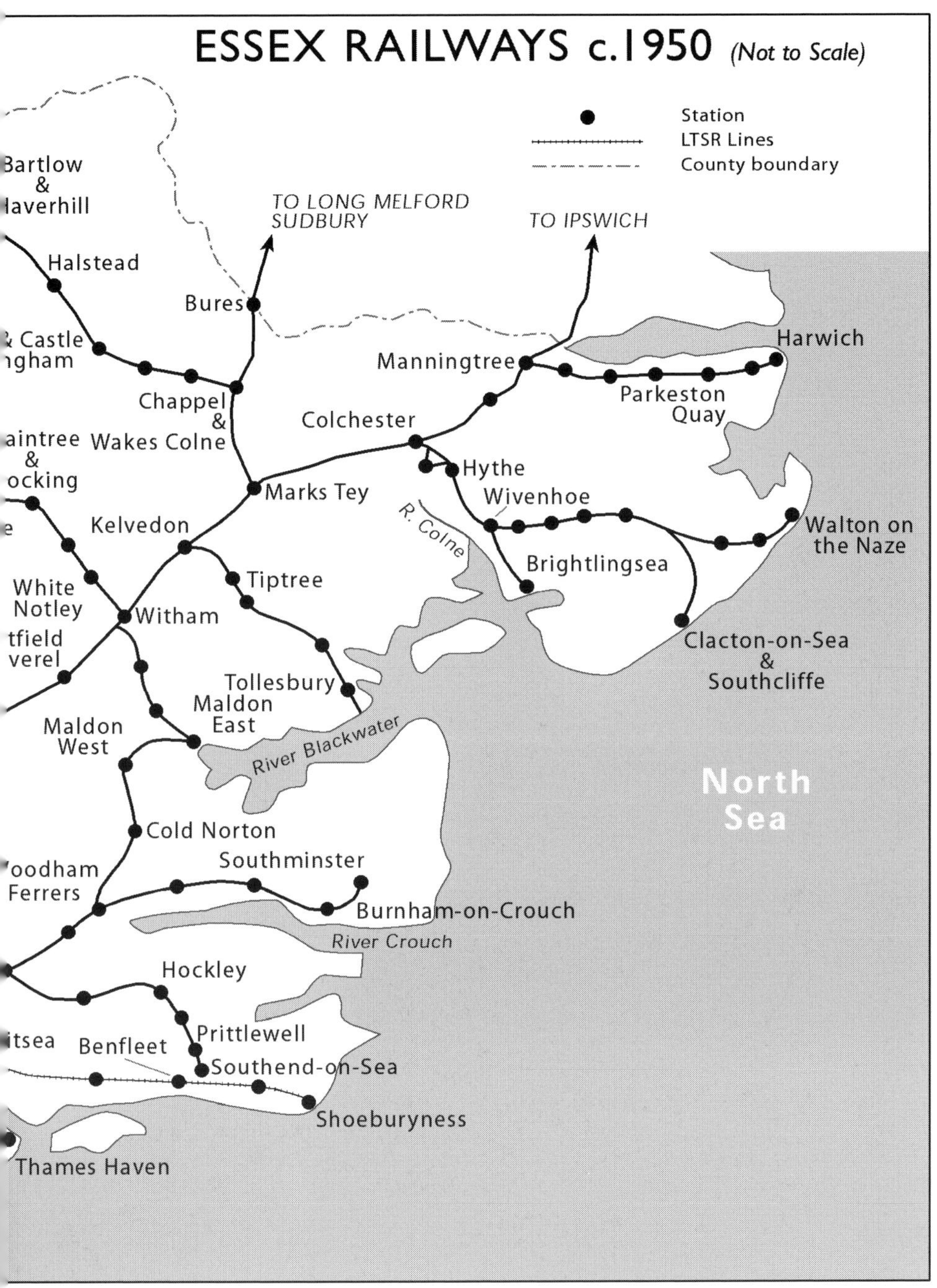

Introduction

Through Cornish mining engineer Richard Trevithick, Britain invented the self-propelled railway locomotive, a technological concept that was to change the face of the globe like nothing else in history had ever done before. One of the principal products of the Industrial Revolution, the steam-powered railway opened up the five continents to trade, creating a new world order based on technology. The railway locomotive laid the foundation of the modern age, and in turn paved the way for the motor car and the aeroplane.

It was on 29 March 1843 that Essex – a beautiful county full of many contrasting landscapes, from weatherboarded villages nestling amidst rolling pastures to inviting sandy shores and bleak estuarine salt marshes – was yanked into the modern age. That was the date when passenger trains began running on the Eastern Counties Railway's (ECR) first main line, over the 51 miles from the London terminus at Shoreditch, later named Bishopsgate, to Colchester.

At first it was built to a non-standard gauge, just like Isambard Kingdom Brunel's Great Western Railway, where the rails were 7 ft apart. The Eastern Counties and the associated Northern & Eastern Railway began with 5 ft gauge, but quickly saw the benefits of standardisation and in October 1844 converted their tracks to the 4 ft 8½ in gauge that became the norm for the British national network.

In 1846, the Eastern Counties became linked to the Eastern Union Railway at Colchester and in 1862 the two companies merged along with a number of other East Anglian railways to form the Great Eastern Railway (GER). By that time many schemes to expand the county's rail network were either underway or proposed.

Many of the new routes were designed to connect outlying rural areas with London, and are still with us today as busy commuter lines, the villages they served having long since been swallowed up to make suburbia. Other railway schemes sought to link with shipping services, creating new ports and waterfronts, and opening up huge swathes of desolate marshland along the north bank of the river Thames to be reclaimed for use by heavy industry, which in turn was served by private railway systems.

The railway brought rapid transport to the masses and created the county's tourist trade. Lines to the coast facilitated the growth of holiday resorts like Clacton-on-Sea, Southend-on-Sea and Walton-on-the-Naze; routes serving these big resorts have survived the years of heavy competition from road traffic.

Of course, many railway schemes failed to reap the rewards that their promoters had promised. Some never got off the ground; others perhaps should never have been built in the form that they were. Cross-country routes, which cut from east to west across the county linking market towns, held out scant hope of ever generating commuter traffic and were left with basic passenger services for most of their existence. Eventually poor patronage meant that they disappeared from the map years before the cost-cutting British Railways chairman Dr Richard Beeching appeared in 1963 to wield his axe. Yet, compared to other shires, Essex fared not too badly under Beeching, largely because so much of the county served by rail was London commuter-belt territory. Nonetheless, many railway routes have gone, some despite vociferous local campaigns to save them, and others with scarcely a whimper.

Many of the closed stations on these lines have been lovingly restored as very desirable private residences, and some of the old trackbeds have survived as footpaths and cycle paths. Elsewhere, nature has been left to reclaim her own, and each year the growth of vegetation gradually resettles the landscape. In the towns, modern redevelopment sweeps away much of what remains at a single stroke, old trackbeds being absorbed into new road schemes as yet another piece of Essex transport history disappears from view.

However, there is still much on the ground for the rambler, antiquarian, railway enthusiast or interested local resident to explore, as this volume will demonstrate. As well as the routes which formed part of the national rail network, this volume also looks at the county's rich variety of private railways, from systems that served heavy industry to lines built purely for pleasure purposes.

Robin Jones

1
London's Docklands

Stratford to North Woolwich
The Silvertown Tramway
The Beckton branch
The Beckton Gas Works Railway
The Port of London Authority and the
Gallions branch

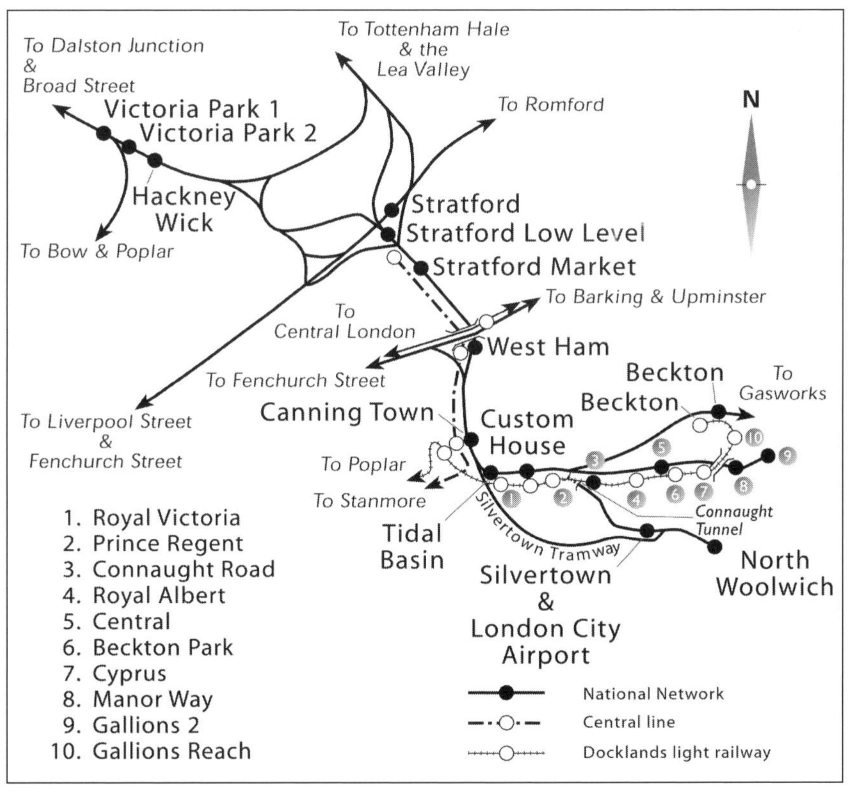

Stratford to North Woolwich

The past 200 years conjure up three distinct images of London's docklands on the north bank of the Thames in Essex. In the early 19th century the areas that today we know as Canning Town, Silvertown, North Woolwich and Beckton were wild, unpopulated marshlands and water meadows. A century later, and the locality was a no-holds-barred hive of heavy industry, centred around huge artificial harbours that had been created to serve the burgeoning port of London, with all the attendant soot, smoke, grime, dirt and basic housing conditions you might expect – and it was all the result of building one railway branch line.

If we fast-forward to the modern age, much of the industry has gone and the docks no longer see ships. However, the very much workaday image of the area still remains, while the dock waterfronts are now home to blocks of luxury flats, with the looming towers of Canary Wharf on the horizon to the west.

We begin our exploration of the lost railways of Essex in this south-western corner of the county. Before the coming of the railway to North Woolwich, the nearest settlement of any importance was Stratford which was first served by the Eastern Counties Railway on 20 June 1839, and was where the company would site its locomotive-building works in 1847. In 1833, a railway line running from Limehouse to the north bank of the Thames opposite the Kent market town of Woolwich was proposed, but the plans came to nothing.

In 1844, George Parker Bidder – who had joined forces with railway pioneers George and Robert Stephenson four years earlier to build the London & Blackwall Railway – unveiled plans for a railway running south from Stratford along the east bank of the river Lea to Bow Creek, where the Lea joins the Thames. His plan involved the creation of a wharf for the off-loading of coal and other commodities which would then be distributed throughout East Anglia by the ECR.

Totalling 2¾ miles in length, this short line opened on 29 April 1846 under the title of the Eastern Counties & Thames Junction Railway, and the terminus was appropriately named Thames Wharf. A further Parliamentary Act empowered the building of a connecting curve at Stratford to allow the branch trains to reach central London, and also a freight spur across the river Lea to the East India Dock Company's pepper warehouses at Blackwall, with a 1-in-30 gradient and very sharp curves. This railway was bought by the Eastern Counties Railway in August 1846.

Thames Wharf became the home of the shipbuilding and ironworks firm of C.J. Mare, which in 1857 became the famous Thames Ironworks, and large numbers of houses for workers sprang up in what became known as Canning Town.

In 1845 an Act of Parliament had been obtained for the North Woolwich Railway to extend the Thames Wharf line across the marshes in 1847 to a lonely and bleak spot on the north bank of the river opposite Woolwich, home of the Royal Arsenal, which at that time lacked a railway connection. The new branch terminus station was therefore named North Woolwich, and although it was never historically part of Woolwich, which lies on the south bank, it was connected to Woolwich Town, later known as South Woolwich, by a steam ferry. It was also bought up by the ECR, later in 1847.

The North Woolwich line opened on 14 June 1847 and passenger services were introduced over the whole route. Two intermediate passenger stations were opened on that day – Stratford Bridge just south of Stratford (later renamed Stratford Market, where the line went below the main road to Romford) and Barking Road, later Canning Town, where it literally met the road to Barking. Traffic boomed at first,

Stratford Market station, originally known as Stratford Bridge and an early closure on the North Woolwich branch. (Author)

but in 1849 the South Eastern Railway opened a direct line to South Woolwich, eliminating the need for a ferry.

The ECR established the Royal Pavilion Gardens next to the terminus at North Woolwich in 1851 in a bid to create day-trip traffic to boost revenue. The venue had a dance hall and other attractions but these were closed down because of rowdiness and the attraction was turned into a public park, named the Royal Victoria Gardens, by London County Council in 1890.

Freight traffic blossomed as more factories were established along the waterfront between the railway and the river. One of the biggest was Silver's Waterproofing Works, which bequeathed the name Silvertown to the housing developments that accommodated its workforce. A

The mothballed North Woolwich line leaving Stratford Low Level is seen to the left, awaiting its conversion to a new branch of the Docklands Light Railway. To the right, a Jubilee Line train departs, while on the overbridge can be seen the closed Stratford Market station building, now in use as offices. (Author)

Silvertown and its station as seen on a typical day in 1948. (Douglas Thompson)

new Stratford (Low Level) station serving the North Woolwich branch was opened on 16 October 1854.

At the start, the very isolated North Woolwich station was served only by a tavern, the Barge House, with a shepherd's dwelling in the immediate locality. However, the ferry pier also served passenger vessels on the Thames, and steamers plying between London and Gravesend called there. Two steam ferries named *Kent* and *Essex* owned by the ECR provided the initial cross-river connection and a third, *Middlesex*, was later added. The railway employed carriages of a 'superior design' on branch services to compensate passengers for the inconvenience of having to change from train to boat.

George Parker Bidder also had interests in property development, and saw the time arriving when London's

F5 class 2-4-2T No 67219 at Stratford (Low Level) on 8 August 1953, forming the 12.45 service from North Woolwich to Palace Gates. (Brian Morrison)

The tidal basin swing bridge carrying the Silvertown Tramway as seen in 1904. (GERS)

historic docklands would no longer be able to cope with booming world trade and the new larger ships that were being built. In conjunction with ECR chairman David Waddington and engineer Samuel Morton Peto, Bidder drew up plans for the Royal Victoria Dock which opened in 1855. The dock was entered from the Thames near Bow Creek, and a swing bridge was build to take the North Woolwich line over it.

It was soon realised that the frequent use of the bridge would delay ships going in and out of the harbour so the dock company built a new bypass route for the North Woolwich branch which would take it around the northern and eastern sides of the dock. The dock company handed this new route over to the ECR, and took the old line in exchange. This original line became known as the Silvertown Tramway, and was retained to serve local factories.

Royal Victoria Dock was the first in the world to have been designed with its own internal railway network, with

Dating from Great Eastern Railway days, Class J68 0-6-0 tank engine No. 68660 awaits the call of duty at Stratford (Low Level) station on 1 June 1956. (R. Cogger/Author's collection)

a sizeable marshalling yard on the north side where wagons were exchanged with the North Woolwich branch. It added greatly to the traffic on the branch, especially with dockers travelling to and from work, and went on to form the basis of a huge network of freight lines serving London's docks. A station was opened on the new branch route at Custom House in late 1855, followed by Tidal Basin in 1858 and Silvertown on 19 June 1863.

Just before the dock was opened, the Eastern Counties Railway had built a connecting spur from the North Woolwich branch at Stratford to the North London Railway at Victoria Park. By virtue of the North London Railway's connections, the spur allowed trains from anywhere in England to run to and from Victoria Dock.

A spur was also provided between Stratford Low Level station and the line to Cambridge, allowing access to the

North Woolwich branch. However, this particular connecting spur ran under the Eastern Counties main line, and the bridge was too low for many types of steam locomotives to pass below. For this reason, for nearly half a century locomotives had to be fitted with shorter chimneys. The easiest method to achieve this was to hinge the chimneys! The problem was eradicated in 1896 when the track was lowered to allow sufficient clearance for locomotives to pass beneath the bridge, regardless of how tall their chimneys were.

In 1858 the London Tilbury & Southend Railway's direct line between Bow and Barking was built, crossing the North Woolwich branch near Stratford Abbey. A connecting spur was also added so that trains could run between North Woolwich and Fenchurch Street via Barking-by-Bow.

As previously stated, the Eastern Counties Railway merged with smaller companies in 1862 to form the Great

Connaught Tunnel on the North Woolwich line, as seen from the rear cab window of the last train on 10 December 2006. (c2c Rail & National Express East Anglia)

Pictured in 2008 is the Gallions Hotel, which stood at the terminus of the short branch line from Custom House. (Author)

Eastern Railway. In 1864 the Victoria Dock Company became part of the London & St Katherine's Dock Company, and as trade boomed ever further in the following years, a newer and much-bigger dock was needed. So in 1880, Royal Albert Dock was opened. It was linked at one end to Victoria Dock and to the Thames at Gallions Reach, slightly downstream of North Woolwich, at the other.

Again, this harbour development left the North Woolwich branch with a swing bridge to cross, impeding the passage of ships into the new dock. And again, the dock company built a diversion for the railway but this time used a tunnel between Custom House and Silvertown, known as Connaught Tunnel. The same arrangement as before persisted: the dock company took the old railway route with the swing bridge in exchange for the new one, but allowed the railway to continue using the old line free of charge for heavier trains which could not be expected to tackle the steep gradients in and out of the tunnel.

When the Royal Albert Dock was opened, the dock company laid its own passenger-carrying branch from the GER at Custom House along the north side of the new harbour to Gallions Reach, where it provided a hotel for the seagoing passengers.

From 1 March 1889 London County Council began providing ferry crossings at North Woolwich free of charge, hitting the trade of the GER, which charged a penny. Nevertheless it was able to keep running its own ferry services for another 19 years.

The railway pier on the Woolwich side of the Thames quickly became disused and was demolished, but the one at North Woolwich survived in use up to the Second World

The pier once served by the North Woolwich branch has lain derelict and fenced off for many years, used only by graffiti artists. (Author)

War as a calling point for river steamers sailing to Southend-on-Sea and Margate. The pier and its rusting graffiti-covered entrance hall still survive, but are now derelict and fenced off.

In 1901, East Ham and West Ham councils introduced electric tram services along the north side of the docks, but this new alternative to the railway appeared to have little or no impact on the North Woolwich branch, for by now the former desolate marshland – the haunt of herons, plovers and bitterns – was heavily urbanised with barely a blade of grass or tree in sight.

On 1 January 1923, the GER became part of the London & North Eastern Railway. The fortunes of the North Woolwich branch began to wane in the face of increased competition from the car, lorry and bus, and in 1937, a trolleybus route was set up from Stratford along the entire length of the branch to the docks. Services on the branch were badly disrupted during the Second World War, notably during the 'Black Saturday' air raid of 7 September 1940, when much of North Woolwich station was destroyed and a stationary train was severely damaged, the docks being a prime Luftwaffe target. After the war, passenger levels dropped still further as dockers were rehoused in prefabs near Beckton and Wanstead Flats away from the principal areas of bomb damage. During the British Railways era, passenger numbers on the North Woolwich branch as well as volumes of goods traffic continued to fall.

Changes in the pattern of freight transportation had an impact on both the branch and the docks it served. British Rail withdrew from single-wagonload traffic in the sixties. Also, the traditional pick-up goods, in which wagons were collected from individual stations, came to an end, as it was decided that such traffic was far better suited for road transportation. The killer blow for the area came with the introduction of container traffic depots at places downstream like Tilbury, a move which closed the local docks almost overnight.

In February 1978, in a bid to revitalise both the rundown branch and area, British Rail announced that all trains from North Woolwich would no longer terminate at Stratford Low Level, but would continue via Victoria Park to Camden via the North London line. In conjunction with the plans for improved services, all stations were rebuilt, although the original terminus building at North Woolwich was earmarked for preservation. The new services began on 14 May 1979, when an island platform at West Ham station was brought into use to provide an interchange with London Underground's District Line.

The service was provided at first by two-car diesel multiple units, which had been the mainstay of the line since the end of steam in the sixties, but in 1985, third-rail electrification took place, and Southern Region electric stock took over, with a new Richmond to North Woolwich service being introduced that May.

In 1986, the branch passed into the control of Network SouthEast and in 1989 it became part of North London Railways during the build-up to the privatisation of the railway network. Silvertown station was given a second lease of life serving the short take-off and landing airport which had been set up alongside King George V dock, and which is now known as London City Airport.

After privatisation, the North Woolwich branch became part of the network operated by Silverlink Trains, although cutbacks, due to lack of passengers, saw it reduced to an unstaffed single-track line. The end came on 10 December 2006, when the last train ran between Stratford Low Level and North Woolwich, a year short of the line's 150th anniversary.

The first section of the Docklands Light Railway, a cut-price but highly efficient system which uses automatic computer-controlled electric trains, unmanned stations and large monorail-like elevated sections, was opened on 31 August 1987. Instead of having drivers, a passenger service agent is responsible for patrolling the train, checking tickets, making announcements and controlling doors, and can also take control of the train in the event of equipment failure and emergencies. The light railway was designed to help regenerate the ailing docklands, and subsequent extensions saw it run north to Stratford, south to Lewisham, west to Bank and east to Beckton and North Woolwich, making a total of nearly 20 miles. A section was built alongside the North Woolwich branch between Canning Town and Custom House, while London Underground's new Jubilee Line was laid side-by-side with the branch between Stratford and Canning Town.

Silvertown station today lies derelict, weeds taking over its tracks, as the branch waits to become part of London's Crossrail link. To the right is the giant Tate & Lyle sugar factory. The Silvertown Tramway diverged from the branch at this point and ran through the triangle of land that is fenced off. (Author)

The closure of the branch came about because of two proposals; firstly, for an extension of the Docklands Light Railway from Canning Town to the new Stratford International, where trains will link with the high-speed Channel Tunnel rail link (High Speed 1) services from St Pancras International to the continent, and secondly, with the easternmost section having been earmarked for London's new Crossrail scheme. The Stratford extension is scheduled to open in 2010, as a key part of a public transport network serving the 2012 Olympic Games. It will have new stations at Star Lane, Abbey Road and Stratford High Street – formerly known as Stratford Market when it served the North London Line before closing on 6 May 1957. Crossrail, a project to build a major new railway beneath central London, was given the go-ahead by Prime Minister Gordon Brown on 5 October 2007. The first trains are scheduled to run in 2017.

The first line will run through a new pair of east-west tunnels linking the Great Western Main Line near Paddington to the Great Eastern Main Line near Stratford. However, a branch from Whitechapel will run below the docklands and appear on the surface at Custom House before following the North Woolwich route, where tracks were still intact but becoming increasingly overgrown in 2008.

The Crossrail branch will run to a point near to North Woolwich station, before disappearing into a new tunnel beneath the Thames to a new station at Woolwich and on to Abbey Wood on the North Kent Line. Crossrail trains will be able to run from Maidenhead and Heathrow in the west to Shenfield and Abbey Wood in the east, with many of the existing stations being rebuilt to accommodate its trains.

However, although the North Woolwich branch as part of the national rail network is now history, all but Silvertown and North Woolwich stations are still open, albeit in a new or altered form, now served by either the Docklands Light Railway or the Jubilee Line, with the prospect of Crossrail to come. Furthermore, the King George V branch of the Docklands Light Railway follows a route that is parallel to the North Woolwich branch, and broadly serves a similar area.

It is certainly a rare example of a lost railway which has since been revived and repackaged in three separate guises, and therefore as a route if not a physical entity, it is far from dead and buried.

Incidentally, two of the original stations on the North Woolwich line have been moved since they opened. Canning Town was moved northwards in 1888, and shifted back south in 1995. Victoria Park, on the connecting North London line, opened in 1856, was relocated in 1866 and closed completely in 1943.

The Silvertown Tramway

The original route of the North Woolwich line which, as stated earlier, was bypassed to avoid the swing bridge over the dock entrance, survived in use until the mid-eighties, serving local factories.

A short distance from Silvertown station, now devoid of its signs following the closure of the North Woolwich line, are the double-track rails of a level crossing still embedded in the road immediately west of the station. Beyond the level crossing the tramway continues as a footpath.

The King George V extension of the Docklands Light Railway broadly follows the route of the Silvertown Tramway, but is carried on a new viaduct between Canning Town and Silvertown before running north via London City Airport. A further extension of the light railway running east

All that remains of the Silvertown Tramway today are the rails of a double-track level crossing near Silvertown station. (Author)

of King George V beneath the Thames to Woolwich Arsenal has been proposed.

Following the decision to upgrade the North Woolwich branch in 1978, a new 'utilitarian' terminus entrance building was provided by British Rail. The original Grade II listed building of 1854 was then closed. However, the old building was acquired by a charitable body, the Passmore Edwards Museum Trust, which restored it with the aim of developing a museum of transport for East London. A large collection of Great Eastern Railway artefacts, varying from station signs and signal arms to crockery and miniature steam locomotives, was acquired for display.

The Old Station Museum, as it was called, was formally opened by HM The Queen Mother on 20 November 1984, after the world's most famous locomotive, LNER A3 Pacific No 4472 *Flying Scotsman*, hauled a special train over the branch. A year later, the museum received a top railway

North Woolwich Old Station Museum is protected by listed-building status and reopened in 1984 as a museum. (Author)

The last steam engine on the North Woolwich line took to the air on 5 June 2008. Watched by owner Bill Parker, Great Eastern saddle tank No 229 was winched out of the Old Station Museum and taken to Gloucestershire. Built in 1876 by Neilson & Co, it served as the Stratford Works shunter at the far end of the North Woolwich line, and was withdrawn as early as 1917. It was sold to the Admiralty for use at Beachley Dock near Chepstow and then resold to the nearby Fairfield Shipyard, where it was preserved. (Geoff Silcock)

heritage award from the transport publishing company Ian Allan for the sympathetic conversion of the building.

However, early ideas to run steam trains over a short section of the branch failed to materialise, and a similar scheme mooted alongside plans to set up a railway training school at North Woolwich in the early 21st century fared no better.

Indeed, by 2008, the museum, now called the North Woolwich Old Station Museum and in the care of the London Borough of Newham, was opened only on Saturday and Sunday afternoons, and its future was shrouded in uncertainty, with many owners taking prime exhibits away to other venues. Its star exhibit, 1876-built Great Eastern Railway 0-4-0 saddle tank No 229, a survivor of the smallest locomotive type on the company's books, which stood on the site of the tiny turntable at the end of the North Woolwich branch, was taken away by owner Bill Parker for restoration at his heritage railway engineering workshops at Bream in the Forest of Dean, being spectacularly craned out of the site on 5 June 2008.

The Beckton branch

It was not only giant docks that were built on the marshland around North Woolwich to serve the mushrooming Victorian capital of Great Britain. In 1867 the Gas, Light & Coke Company applied for Parliamentary sanction to build a new gasworks south-west of Barking Creek to serve the whole of London. Beckton Gasworks began production on 25 November 1870 and the following year the company obtained permission for a two-mile branch railway to run from the North Woolwich line east of Custom House station to a terminus station built next to the gasworks, from where it served the sprawling internal railway system.

Freight trains to the gasworks began on 14 October 1872, with workmen's trains being introduced on 17 March 1873. A station was built close to the works entrance in Winsor Terrace, and on 18 March 1874 it was opened to passengers, with the Beckton branch being leased to the Great Eastern Railway. The station boasted a single platform with a signal box, shelter and booking office. A separate private station, Beckton Gas Works, was situated within the works and operated until just after the turn of the century. Passenger services on the Beckton branch were hit by the building of the Barking bypass in 1927, making car journeys into the city easier, and also by a direct bus connection from Stratford. Beckton also suffered from the Blitz, and passenger services were finally withdrawn on 29 December 1940.

Freight continued on the branch however, with new sidings built to accommodate coal trains as the German

The Docklands Light Railway depot at Beckton. Part of the light railway near here runs on the trackbed of the steam-era Beckton branch. (Transport for London)

bombing had made it difficult to deliver coal by sea (the gasworks had a pier on its half-mile of river frontage).

The advent of North Sea gas finally killed off the works by the late sixties. The final coal train arrived at Beckton on 16 April 1969 with gas production ending two months later. The last train from the gasworks, carrying a consignment of pitch from the by-product works, ran on 1 June 1970, and the line was officially closed the following February with all of the track lifted by 1973. The site of the terminus station is now buried beneath a roundabout in Royal Docks Road.

Beckton is again served by rail, in the form of the Docklands Light Railway, a branch of which occupies about 100 yards of the old line in Beckton itself. A depot for the light railway stands on part of the gasworks site.

The Beckton Gas Works Railway

Beckton Gas Works was built on the north bank level of the Thames at Gallions Reach to manufacture gas and coke from coal, and was the biggest works of its kind in the world.

Built to supply gas to London, at one stage it covered 360 acres. The site to the west of Barking Creek was chosen because it would allow the building of deep-water piers for direct unloading of coal from steam colliers from Durham. In the thirties, a million tons of coal were loaded each year on average, and another 750,000 tons were transhipped to barges which took the coal elsewhere. Not only was it served by a branch line of its own, as already described, but it also had a massive internal railway network which at its peak had a track mileage of 41 miles, all standard gauge and fully signalled, with 14 signal boxes. The system was so huge that 50 engines were used to operate it. It even had its own locomotive works which not only maintained locomotives but in 1902 built two new ones by itself. The locomotive works and wagon shops alone employed 600 men at one stage.

The locomotives were mainly 0-4-0 saddle and side tanks, built to a low height and mostly without cabs so that they could operate within the very small loading gauge of 6 ft 6 ins around the works. Mostly constructed by Neilson of Glasgow between 1893 and 1896, they were nicknamed Jumbos.

There was also a smaller associated railway system serving the company's by-product works. Following the invention of coal gas early in the 19th century, it was discovered that numerous chemicals and by-products could be obtained during the purifying stages, notably coal tar, ammonia and sulphuric acid. In the 1870s the Silvertown-based company Burt, Boulton & Haywood distilled 12

One sole gasholder remains on the skyline at Beckton today showing where the great gas works and its massive internal railway system once operated. (Author)

Beckton Gas Works No 1 is a Neilson 0-4-0 well tank built in 1870 and is pictured on site. (Andrew Neale collection)

Beckton Gas Works No 1 is now preserved at the Penrhyn Castle Industrial Railway Museum near Bangor in North Wales. (National Trust)

million gallons of coal tar each year to produce the ingredients for disinfectants, insecticides and dyes. Other local factories used the sulphur to produce fertilisers.

The gas company decided it could make more money by making these by-products itself, and opened a purpose-built chemical works in 1879. It was known for many years as the Tar & Liquor works. It had 15 locomotives to serve its internal system, all of them numbered in a different sequence from those on the gas works lines. Several fireless locomotives were used in order to reduce the risk of explosions amongst volatile chemicals. These were basically the same as an 'ordinary' steam engine, but had a large insulated pressure tank instead of a boiler, and it was charged with high-pressure steam produced by a conventional stationary boiler sited well away from the chemical works.

Diesels replaced steam locomotives on the internal systems in the late fifties, although one 0-4-0 side tank was kept until March 1967 to serve the final retort house in operation at the gas works. The gas works site has been largely redeveloped and is now occupied by an industrial estate, the Beckton Retail Park and Gallions Reach Shopping Park. By 2008, a lone gasholder towered over the once-sprawling site now bisected by modern roads.

Two of the gas works saddle tanks, dating from 1892 and 1896 respectively, are preserved at Bressingham Steam Museum at Diss in Norfolk, while an earlier Neilson 0-4-0 well tank, No 1 in the fleet and dating from 1870, is on static display at the Penrhyn Castle Industrial Railway Museum near Bangor in North Wales.

Interestingly, the works site was used for location filming on several occasions, notably in 1975 for the John Wayne film *Brannigan*, in 1981 for the James Bond movie *For Your Eyes Only* and for Stanley Kubrick's *Full Metal Jacket* in 1987.

Port of London Authority locomotives waiting for their next job. (Author's collection)

The Port of London Authority and the Gallions branch

As well as the passenger-carrying lines around London's docklands, the Port of London Authority, largely through its predecessors, developed a labyrinthine system of standard-gauge freight lines to serve the dockyards on the north bank of the Thames.

As already stated, the Royal Victoria Dock was built with an extensive internal railway system to serve it. A locomotive depot was built at the eastern end of the dock, which had no fewer than six signal boxes to control it. The port's own railway linked the docks, sheds and warehouses with the national railway network and eventually totalled 140 miles of track. By the thirties, the port had built up a fleet of 27 steam locomotives, mainly 0-4-0s and 0-6-0s, but towards the end of the fifties, steam had begun to give way to diesel.

The last train to North Woolwich was formed by Silverlink Metro electric multiple unit No 313101 on 10 December 2006. (c2c Rail & National Express East Anglia)

The Port of London Authority's freight-only lines were often pressed into service to handle boat-train traffic, some ships berthing in the Royal Victoria Dock, and others in the King George V dock. The boat trains would leave the North Woolwich branch at Albert Dock Junction, and would engage a dock pilotman to guide the engine driver along the waterfront lines.

The port was also responsible for building one significant and very successful passenger-carrying branch of the North Woolwich line. The Royal Albert Dock Company had statutory rights under the London & St Katharine Dock Act of 1882 to build a railway for both passengers and parcels from the North Woolwich line to Gallions Reach, on the northern side of the new dock. Under the provisions of the act, the company was obliged to run daily trains over the mile-and-two-thirds-long branch for the conveyance of workmen.

The Gallions branch, which diverted from the North Woolwich line slightly to the east of Custom House station, saw its first passenger trains on 3 August 1880, when services ran between Albert Dock Junction and Central station. These services were extended to the terminus at Gallions later that year, with the company hiring the bay platform at Custom House as a western terminus. There were other intermediate stations at Connaught Road and Manor Way. The line between Connaught Road and Central was initially single track, but was doubled on 14 November 1881 to cope with demand.

The London & St Katharine Docks Company bought three second-hand locomotives and passenger carriages to run with half-hourly trains during the working day, stepping services up to three per day in 1881, when hourly through trains to Fenchurch Street began.

At the eastern terminus, the Gallions Hotel was built to provide accommodation for ship passengers. The front door of the hotel opened directly on to the platform.

The original Gallions station was closed on 12 December 1886 because the line needed to be slightly diverted to allow for alterations to the dock. A replacement and bigger station 275 yards to the east was opened, with Great Eastern Railway trains operating out of platform 1 and the dock company's trains out of platform 2. The track continued beyond the station to a coal wharf and pier at Gallions Reach.

The Great Eastern Railway took over the running of local services from Custom House on 1 July 1896, but the line continued to be manned by port staff. Services on the Gallions branch reached the height of their popularity around 1900, when there were more than 50 passenger trains a day over the short branch, making the route a major success. The dock company became part of the Port of London Authority on 31 March 1909.

During 1918, a special wartime service to Gallions was operated for munitions workers brought by ferry from Woolwich Arsenal on the far side of the river.

The stations at Gallions and Manor Way were rebuilt in the mid twenties. The local shuttle services from Custom House to Gallions ceased on 6 June 1932, Sunday trains having ended in June 1915.

The Gallions line was badly damaged during the first major air raid of the Blitz on 7 September 1940, and passenger trains never ran over it again. The branch was repaired for the storage of wagons, a practice which continued until the mid-1960s, despite it being officially abandoned under the legislation of 1950. Much of the track was lifted in the late sixties, but sections were still intact at Gallions in 1974.

Virtually all traces of the original Gallions branch have disappeared, although a section of the Beckton line of the Docklands Light Railway follows part of its route between Manor Way and Gallions, albeit on a new trackbed. The Grade II-listed hotel, now surrounded by luxury apartment blocks, survives and has undergone renovation.

The Port of London Authority Railways dieselised en bloc in 1961, replacing the large assortment of steam locomotives which made up its fleet with Yorkshire Engine Company diesel hydraulic locomotives. The system closed in 1970, with the diesels being sold into industry elsewhere.

2
The Green Shire beyond the Great Forest

The Epping Ongar Railway

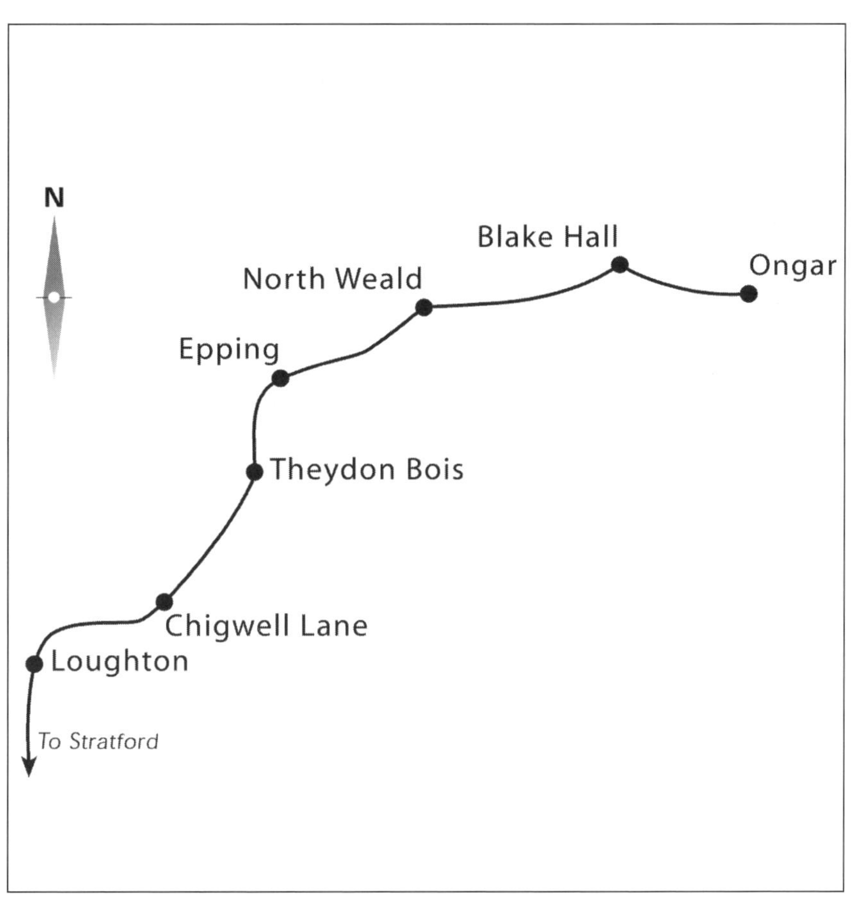

Nobody seems to have ever really known what to do with the branch line from Epping to Chipping Ongar, or plain old Ongar as it has been known ever since the railway arrived there. Does it hold unlocked potential as a commuter route to London, as a major tourist attraction, should it have been absorbed into the London Underground system – or should it never have been built at all?

Planned as part of a much longer route from London into deepest Essex which was never built, the section north of Essex struggled badly in its final decades to pay its way. Built as a steam-operated line, it became part of the electrified London Underground network – the distinctive red tube trains running through open fields in virgin countryside a world away from the city tunnels and suburbia – and is a very rare example of part of that system to close in modern times. Although now closed it continues to generate controversy and debate, right up to the present day, having been partially reopened for heritage operations.

A meeting of two cultures: a steam-hauled service bound for Ongar leaves Epping on 1 June 1956, while classic Underground stock forms a southbound train, in the year before the northernmost section was electrified too. (R. Coggar, author's collection)

F6 tank engine No 67218 waits to depart from Ongar, behind the long-demolished signal box. (Epping Ongar Railway Society)

The line had its origins in a scheme proposed in 1845 by the London & Blackwall Railway to link the city with the towns of Loughton and Epping at the edge of the great green swathe of Epping Forest. Fearing competition, the Eastern Counties Railway did not warm to the plan and refused the LBR permission to operate in and out of Stratford. Instead, the ECR agreed to build its own line and after several schemes were proposed, on 8 July 1853, it obtained Royal Assent to create a route from Stratford to Woodford and Loughton. The double-track line opened on 22 August 1856, with stations at Low Leyton, Leytonstone, Snaresbrook, George Lane, Woodford, Buckhurst Hill and Loughton.

In 1859, a separate concern, the Epping Railways Company, received Parliamentary approval to extend the line from Loughton to Epping and Chipping Ongar, and in the following year, obtained further powers to extend it through the heart of Essex to Dunmow. An extension as far as Bury St Edmunds was also briefly mooted.

The ECR was horrified about the proposed incursion into its territory, and in 1861 won the right to build a line between Braintree and Bishop's Stortford via Dunmow – more of that in a chapter to follow – thereby blocking the rival scheme. The rivalry ended in July and August 1862, when the Epping Railways Company was taken over by the ECR, which then amalgamated with the Eastern Union Railway to form the Great Eastern Railway. The plans for the line from Ongar to Dunmow were then abandoned. Had it gone ahead, the map of that part of Essex would certainly look very different today.

On 29 August 1862, the GER appointed engineer Thomas Brassey to build the Loughton to Ongar section, with intermediate stations at Chigwell Road (now known as Debden) and Theydon Bois, tapping into the Victorian

End of the line: a 1950s scene shows F5 tank engine No 67203 at Ongar. Note how the line ends abruptly in a cutting, showing that Ongar was not the intended final destination. (Epping Ongar Railway Society)

tourist market for day trippers to Epping Forest. Because the area surrounding the forest was then sparsely populated, only a single-track line was deemed necessary, but passing loops were installed at Theydon Bois and Epping, beyond which there were further intermediate stations at North Weald and the lonely outpost of Blake Hall, named after a nearby mansion.

There were several stiff gradients, and the section east of Epping, 340 ft above sea level, was the highest point on the whole GER system for many years. The only major engineering work was the five-arch Cripsey Brook viaduct immediately to the west of Ongar station. The terminus at Ongar was built as a through station because the GER wanted the option of extending further east, perhaps to its main line at Chelmsford. Again, an extension was never built.

The Loughton to Ongar section opened on 24 April 1865 to minimal celebrations, with a cadet corps from a local grammar school saluting the first arrival with a rifle volley on Ongar platform. Sadly, the last train of the day came to an abrupt end when the locomotive became derailed at North Weald. There were no injuries, but passengers set to arrive in Ongar at 9.30 pm did not get there until 5 am!

Once Ongar was opened, the original terminus at Loughton was closed and sold off, and a replacement station was built to serve the town. Coal, general goods and milk were the main commodities carried on the line. Increased patronage of the line led to doubling of the track between Loughton and Epping – but no further. Fifty trains ran between London and Loughton each day, with another 22 continuing to Epping and just 14 more to Ongar.

There was a small engine shed and a goods shed at Ongar, although the turntable was taken out in 1917, leaving locomotives to either run round their trains, or services to be run on a push-pull basis.

Ongar's small steam shed as pictured in June 1938. (Author's collection)

The GER had toyed with the idea of electrifying part of its system, but never had the chance to put any of its ideas into practice before the Grouping of 1923, when it became part of the London & North Eastern Railway. In 1933, the London Passenger Transport Board, later to become London Transport, was established and two years later it announced its New Works Programme.

The massive and far-reaching programme involved both the government and other main line railway companies and aimed to electrify main line track and work together to reduce costs while providing the public with an improved service. However, in the early stages, the government did not support electrification.

The programme included the extension of the underground system's Central Line beyond its existing terminus at Liverpool Street through a tunnel to Stratford. There it would offer an interchange with LNER services, before again disappearing into another tunnel and reappearing above ground to join the line to Epping and

The Loughton to Epping section of the original route as built has remained open. Although now part of London Underground, the architecture of Theydon Bois station reveals its steam era past. (Author)

Great Eastern Railway F5 2-4-2 tank No 67202 at Epping shed in 1950, still providing sterling service in the early days of British Railways. (Epping Ongar Railway Society)

Ongar. However when the Second World War broke out in 1939 these extensions to the Central Line were postponed, while the services between Ongar and London were cut to just seven trains per day.

The Central Line extension programme resumed immediately after the end of the war, and the underground reached Leytonstone in 1946, Woodford in 1947 and Loughton in 1948, with electric trains replacing steam on this route. North of Loughton, a steam-hauled shuttle service continued to operate to Ongar and a passing loop was installed at North Weald on 14 August 1949 to allow more trains to operate. Postwar housing schemes and the demand for through services led to the electrification of the line to Epping, which became served by the Central Line on 25 September 1949.

At the nationalisation of the railways in 1948, the assets of both the old railway companies and London Transport were divided amongst new executive bodies. The new London Transport Executive took over the former London Transport assets including the line from Leyton to Loughton. The London Transport Executive was also handed control of the Epping to Ongar section, and hired the steam trains from British Railways' Eastern Region which were still run on a push-pull basis, hauled by GER F5 2-4-2 tank engines.

Steam continued to haul passenger trains between Epping and Ongar until 1957 when the single-track line was electrified, tube trains running over it from 18 November that year. However, the electrification of this northernmost section was done on the cheap, with power supply limitations meaning that the section had to be self-contained, with no through running. Passengers had to change trains at Epping, a factor which was clearly a great discouragement to Ongar commuters. A 20-minute passenger service ran between Epping and Ongar, although

A pre-electrification scene from the Ongar line in the early 1950s, with F5 tank No 67213 waiting in a siding with its passenger train, behind a private-owner coal wagon. (Epping Ongar Railway Society)

goods trains continued to be hauled over the line by steam in the form of classic GER J15 0-6-0 tender locomotives.

However, this was the era in which we were told we had never had it so good, and the car became king. New housing estates sprang up at Chipping Ongar, but they failed to generate the expected levels of passenger numbers for the railway, travellers also being put off by the slow journey to cover just six-and-a-half-miles. Falling passenger numbers led to Blake Hall station being closed on Sundays from 17 October 1966 when a reduced weekday timetable was implemented. Four years later, London Transport announced plans to close the Epping to Ongar section altogether. Eventually Essex County Council agreed to subsidise the section, but further declining passenger numbers led to the decommissioning of the passing loop and signal box at North Weald in 1976, and the subsidy being withdrawn the following year.

The final electric service on the line passes Blake Hall, the least patronised of all London Underground stations when it closed. (Epping Ongar Railway Society)

Another failed attempt to close the line came in 1980 but victory was short-lived. Blake Hall station was closed completely on 31 October 1981, when services on the rest of the section north of Epping were also reduced. Blake Hall was not only the worst patronised station on the whole of the underground system, but was said to have the lowest number of passengers on any underground system anywhere in the world. Following closure, its platforms were removed, but the station acquired listed-building status and has been restored as a private house.

In a renewed bid to justify the survival of the Epping-Ongar section, a brave attempt was made in 1989 to run an all-day service. However, it proved unsuccessful and London Transport finally closed it on 30 September 1994, with fewer than 100 passengers a day using the line.

Despite the poor passenger levels on the Epping to Ongar

The final public train on the Epping-Ongar line is seen passing through North Weald on 30 September 1994. (Epping Ongar Railway Society)

section, many were convinced that given the will, a fair wind, and a major pruning of costs, there could yet be value in running commuter services and so the government sought a private operator for it.

Two rival parties emerged. One was a commercial outfit known as Pilot Developments which promised to reintroduce commuter trains. Pilot was opposed by an enthusiast group called the Ongar Railway Preservation Society, which argued that commuter trains were not viable, but that a heritage/tourist service could be run, using steam, and tabled a £325,000 bid to buy the line and run it as a charity. However, the enthusiast lobby were dismayed in autumn 1998 when Labour Transport Minister Glenda Jackson's administration sold the line to Pilot for an undisclosed sum.

Despite assurances by Pilot that commuter services would restart within five years of the purchase, no such trains ever ran. The company was refused permission to run trains into Epping station because of improved service frequencies on the Central Line, while building a new Epping station to the immediate north was deemed impractical.

Pilot then removed the electrified rails from the branch, saying it had done so because of the damage that had been caused by burrowing rabbits. However, the running line was repaired and Pilot bought two diesel multiple units to run services over it, lowering the track beneath the M11 motorway bridge (built, of course, since the steam era) to allow stock taller than underground units to pass beneath it.

One of the Finnish main line engines which have been stored at Ongar station in recent times but which are too big to run on any British line. (Author)

Businessman Nigel Sill, Pilot's operations manager, brought four steam locomotives to Ongar for display, but they were built to run on the 5 ft gauge main line in Finland (ironically the same gauge as the Eastern Counties Railway started with) rather than the 4 ft 8½ ins British and western European standard gauge, and so could not be used on the branch. He had successfully operated tourist trains in Finland, and the four had been imported to England for an abortive scheme to build a 5 ft gauge line at the Spirit of the West American wild west theme park near St Columb in Cornwall. A fifth, operational, Finnish engine was briefly brought to Ongar in 2006 and steamed on a short length of track for one weekend.

A second enthusiast body, the Epping Ongar Railway Volunteer Society, was later formed to support the railway's owners. On 3 October 2004, the new society launched its first passenger trips between Ongar and North Weald stations using one of the two diesel multiple units. The inaugural run paved the way for further 'heritage' trips at weekends on a regular basis.

The goods yard at Ongar was eventually sold to a housing developer and in early 2008, bus operator Roger Wright, who at one time owned Blue Triangle Buses, bought out the other partners in Epping Ongar Railway (Holdings) Ltd, leaving him as sole owner of the railway, and pledging to fully refurbish the track for more heritage trains to be run, including steam services.

In 2000, members of the Ongar Railway Preservation Society formed the Holden F5 Steam Locomotive Trust to build, in Essex, a new example of the F5 2-4-2 tank engines which were the last steam engines to haul passenger trains to Ongar in 1957. None had survived into preservation.

Preservationists have not ignored the line's electric heritage. Cravens Heritage Trains, a group which has preserved two complete vintage London Underground

Teenagers from 159 countries celebrated the centenary of scouting at the 21st World Scout Jamboree at Hylands Park in Chelmsford in July and August 2007, with many groups carrying out volunteer work at projects around Essex. One such group is seen washing down the Epping Ongar Railway's diesel multiple unit at Ongar station. (Author)

trains, has leased the disused Epping signal cabin which will be restored to 1940s condition.

With the rising price of petrol, the congestion charge in central London, and increasing pressure for more homes around the capital, it would be foolish to predict that the regular passenger-carrying days of the Ongar branch are over yet.

3
Rural Byways and Borderland Backwaters

The Saffron Walden Railway
The Elsenham & Thaxted Light Railway

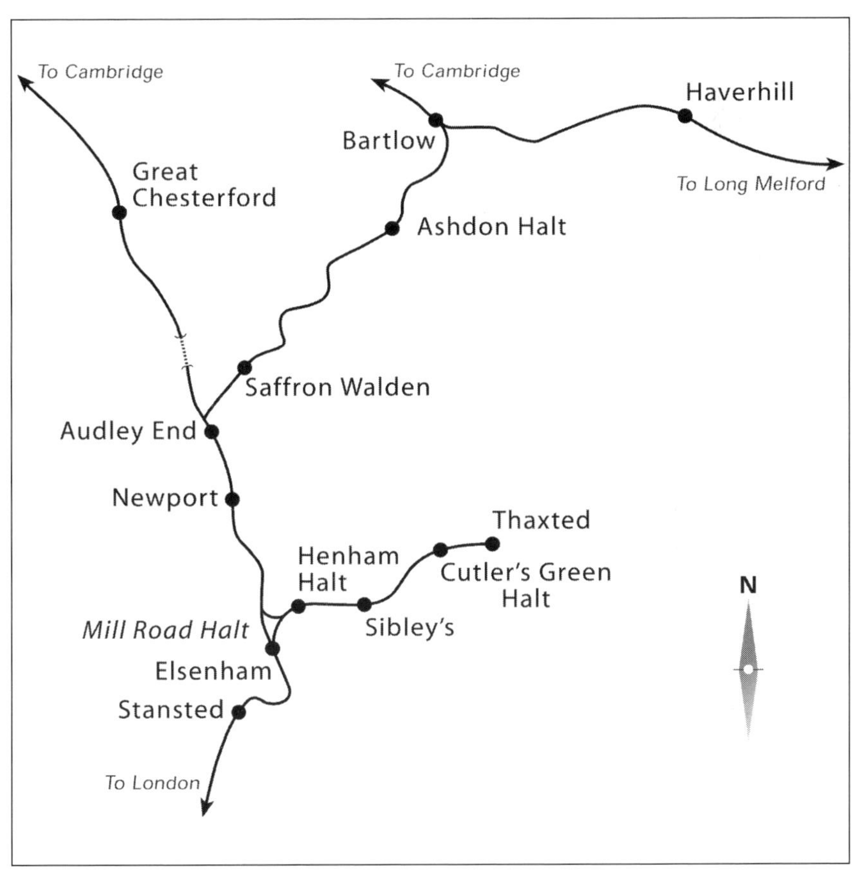

The Saffron Walden Railway

With its many picturesque medieval buildings, including the biggest church in Essex, Saffron Walden is easily one of the finest market towns in the county. Walden Abbey, a priory, was founded here around 1136. In the 16th and 17th centuries a brisk business developed in growing the saffron crocus, the flower of which was used in medicines, perfumes, aphrodisiacs and yellow dyes – hence the modern name of the town.

The saffron industry was replaced by brewing in the early 19th century, and by the 1830s there were 30 breweries and maltings in the town. There was much excitement when, in 1835, the town was surveyed as part of a route for a railway from London to Cambridge. However, local landowner Lord Braybrooke did not want a station sited in Saffron Walden, and so one had to be built two miles away at Audley End.

The town soon came to realise that this decision was a big mistake, for by this time, no railway meant no prosperity. Accordingly, the population dwindled from more than 5,000 to around 4,700 as people moved out looking for work. A public meeting held in 1860 led to a proposal being made to the Eastern Counties Railway for a branch line from Audley End to Saffron Walden. Sufficient local finance was made available and the Saffron Walden Railway Act received royal assent on 22 July 1861.

Such was the clamour for the town to have its own rail link that before work started plans were drawn up for a northern extension to the Stour Valley line between Cambridge and Sudbury, with a junction at Bartlow. Building work on the first section from Audley End began on 18 May 1863, a fortnight before the extension was approved. The branch to Saffron Walden was opened on 23 November 1865. The extension to Bartlow, which needed cuttings and embankments as it ran through hillier terrain, opened on 26 October 1866.

Despite the enthusiasm for the line, passenger numbers were disappointing from the start, and more unpopularity was caused by the imposition of a 10 mph speed limit.

The Saffron Walden Railway Company was bought on 1 January 1877 by the Great Eastern who introduced a through service to London. In the 1880s, there were seven trains a day from Audley End, with four going through to Bartlow. Goods traffic increased steadily, and boomed during the First World War when more agricultural produce was despatched to make up for the loss of imported foreign food.

After the war, many military lorries and vans were privately bought by demobilised troops wanting to set up their own businesses. This was a countrywide phenomenon, but it impacted on rural backwaters like the Saffron Walden

A typical branch train pulls into Saffron Walden station. (Lens of Sutton)

branch, with goods traffic switching gradually from rail to road.

At Saffron Walden, a long siding ran under South Road bridge to the Gas House siding and the Anglo American Oil Company's tanks. Tracks led from here to an engine shed and turntable and two sidings serving an iron and brass foundry, loading dock, and in the 19th century, a cement works. The goods yard had a large goods shed, cattle pens, coal wharves and offices.

The decline in freight traffic which occurred as a result of the 1926 General Strike dealt a sizeable blow to the branch's finances, although passenger trade improved in the 1930s when more ramblers and day trippers from London were carried, and by 1937, there were 18 daily trains from Audley End to Saffron Walden, seven going through to Bartlow.

Locomotives on branch duties were predominantly tank engines including Great Northern Railway C12 class 4-4-2s, Great Eastern Railway N7 0-6-2s displaced from London suburban services and North Eastern Railway G5 0-4-4s. Evacuees from the capital filled the branch line trains at the start of the Second World War and freight traffic also picked up with the introduction of petrol rationing.

German-built diesel railbuses were introduced by British Railways on the line in 1958 at the start of nationwide plans to switch from steam to 'modern' traction, but despite their success in cutting operating costs, Dr Richard Beeching still listed the branch for closure in his infamous report of 1963 which sounded the death knell for numerous rural routes across Britain. Passenger services were withdrawn from the whole line on 7 September 1964 and freight from 28 December 1964.

The last piece of track was lifted in 1970 ... but not before steam returned for one last time. London, Midland & Scottish Railway's 'Black Five' 4-6-0 No 44871 was brought to Bartlow station for the location filming of the 1969 hit

A diesel railbus calls at the Audley End line's Bartlow station in the line's twilight years. (Bevan Price)

One of the last steam locomotives run under British Railways had short-lived stardom in this scene from The Virgin Soldiers *filmed at Bartlow, before being scrapped. (Tim Simpson)*

movie *The Virgin Soldiers*. Disguised as a freelance 'Malaysian locomotive' and fitted with side tanks and a headlight to give it a tropical appearance, it was lifted by crane into a hole and surrounded by twisted lengths of track.

The locomotive was one of three 'Black Fives' that had hauled the last-ever steam train over the national network by British Rail, the 'Fifteen Guinea Special' of 11 August 1968 a few weeks before. It was afterwards bought privately for preservation. Sadly, after the filming contract was over, the new owner could not afford the sky-high charges which were demanded for moving it again, and in desperation sold it to a scrap dealer to be cut up on site, wiping away a significant piece of UK railway history at a stroke.

The junction at Audley End was severed from the network by June 1965, and the branch station shelter now serves as a

The Audley End branch platform survives in transport use – as a bike rack! (Author)

Saffron Walden station has been converted into two private residences. (Author)

A surviving enamel sign from Audley End station, now in Mangapps Railway Museum. (Author)

bicycle rack and place to park motorbikes for passengers using the adjacent main line station.

With Saffron Walden now being a very desirable place to live, the population has soared beyond 15,000, but residents accept that if they want to use the train, they must first use some other form of transport to reach Audley End on the now-electrified Cambridge line, and that there is all but no chance their railway will ever return, if only because of the amount of building that has taken place on the trackbed.

The substantial Saffron Walden station building once comprising the stationmaster's house, booking office and waiting room has survived and has been converted into two attractive private residences.

Bartlow's station building, which served the Stour Valley line, has been converted into a private house named *The Booking Hall*. The branch line had a separate station alongside, a platform 25 yards short of the junction and a wooden hut for a waiting shelter. A footpath linked the platform to the main line station.

The Elsenham & Thaxted Light Railway

If ever a railway in Essex epitomised the concept of an obscure branch line serving a sleepy rural inland backwater, this was it. The Elsenham & Thaxted Light Railway was very much a local affair. Known as the 'Farmers' Line', it was opened on 1 April 1913, long after the great period of British railway building had ended, and just before motor transport was to present a serious alternative. Indeed, it was the last major railway project in Essex.

Proposed as early as 1896 by Sir Walter Gilbey of Elsenham, the five-and-a-half-mile route was designed to provide effective transport for local farms, taking produce

A contemporary postcard depiction of the Thaxted branch. (Author's collection)

to market. It was built under the provisions of the 1896 Light Railways Act, which, broadly speaking, allowed 'minimalist' branch lines to be built to link sparsely-populated rural areas, which the main railway companies had deemed economically unjustifiable, to the national network. One of the main aims was to relieve the impact of agricultural depression in the countryside, creating work for local people.

Such 'light' railways were built on the cheap, made planning permission easier, and offered government grant aid council rates reductions, but were limited to certain types of locomotive and had a speed restriction of 25 mph. Indeed, Britain's preserved railways today operate under provisions laid down in such Light Railway Orders.

Thaxted, one of the principal picture-postcard towns in north-east Essex, was described in the Domesday Book of 1086 as Tachesteda, meaning 'the place where thatch was got.' It has many splendid buildings including the Guildhall, Horham Hall and John Webb's windmill. In former times, Thaxted was a local centre for cutlery manufacture until it lost the ability to compete with Sheffield. In the late 19th century, it lay six miles from the nearest railway station, and many local people believed that its fortunes would change again only if it had its own branch line.

As originally proposed, it was intended to continue the line beyond Thaxted to Great Bardfield, a distance of more than ten miles from Elsenham. However, the money to build the whole line never materialised: while the Great Eastern Railway had agreed to pay half the cost of building the line, and a grant of £33,000 was made available by the Treasury, insufficient local capital was raised.

Lack of funds led to a delay between the granting of the Light Railway Order in 1906 for the Thaxted branch and the start of building work in 1911. The GER agreed to build the line, with Sir Walter cutting the first sod at Thaxted on 25 July that year.

Tragedy befell the construction team on 1 July 1912, when a platelayer who had been riding with a gang of 30 on a coal tender was crushed, after the brakes failed and the locomotive smashed into a rake of ballast trucks.

Sir Walter returned to perform the official opening ceremony on 1 April 1913, and the Great Eastern ran a special train from Liverpool Street to mark the occasion. The line left the GER's Liverpool Street to Cambridge route at Elsenham, where the branch had a small goods yard, and finished a mile away from Thaxted parish church, so that an expensive bridge over the river Chelmer would not have to be built to take it further into town. The town's station comprised a single platform with a run-round loop and a corrugated-iron engine shed.

There were very basic intermediate stops at Mill Road

Sibley's, a typical cut-price halt on the Thaxted line. (GERS/John Baker collection)

Halt, Henham Halt, Sibley's for Chickney & Broxted and Cutler's Green Halt. At Sibley's, wagons on the goods loop were shunted by an engine on the running line using a towrope, it taking ten minutes to manoeuvre them so that they could be attached to the train. Cutler's Green Halt was just a low cinder platform with an old coach body for a waiting room.

Typical of light railways, the branch had few major earthworks to tackle large gradients, ungated level crossings protected only by cattle grids (then newly-imported from Canada) and just one bridge. There were no signals, as only one engine in steam was allowed at any one time. Trains slowed to 10 mph for the crossings and halts which were request stops. The trains comprised a mixture of passenger coaches and goods wagons.

George Lee, a Thaxted magistrate who ran a large sweet factory in the town, and had bemoaned the lack of a railway connection, died a fortnight after seeing the branch finally open.

Elsenham, the start of the journey to Thaxted, is now a commuter station on the electrified London to Cambridge line. (Author)

At first there were five trains to Thaxted each day, increasing to seven in the midweek in the 1930s. The locomotives were usually GER 0-6-0 tank engines of the J67, J68 and J69 classes, with occasional visits by J15 tender engines, and coaches were GER six-wheeled wooden-bodied carriages which had become largely obsolete elsewhere.

The line became part of the London & North Eastern Railway at the Grouping of the railways, which came into effect on 1 January 1923. Remarkably, despite its slow trains and poor passenger connections, it was to survive in the face of more convenient road transport for another three decades.

Trains were cut to two a day during the Second World War, but were restored to four or five afterwards. However, few passengers were carried, and when a locomotive derailed in the early fifties leaving the handful on board to be taken on by taxi, the usefulness of the line was called into question. Eastern National buses successfully applied to run a service from Bishop's Stortford to Thaxted. This signalled the end of the line, with the final passengers being carried on 13 September 1952.

It was a sad day for guard Mr P. Reeve, who had worked on the branch since it opened in 1913, and who was presented with a pewter tankard for his long service. Final closure came when goods services were withdrawn from Thaxted and Sibley's on 1 June 1953.

The main station building at Thaxted, the engine shed and water tank all survive within a builder's yard. No trace of the halts survives.

Thaxted, incidentally, is famous as the home of the British composer Gustav Holst, who wrote *The Planets*, and of the novelist Diana Wynne Jones. Its population today is around 2,600.

Thaxted station, which is now surrounded by a builder's yard. (GERS/John Baker collection)

4
Down the Thames Estuary

The Corringham Light Railway
The Thames Haven branch
Tilbury Riverside
Samuel Williams' wharves lines
Chalk and cement
The Thames marshes tip railways

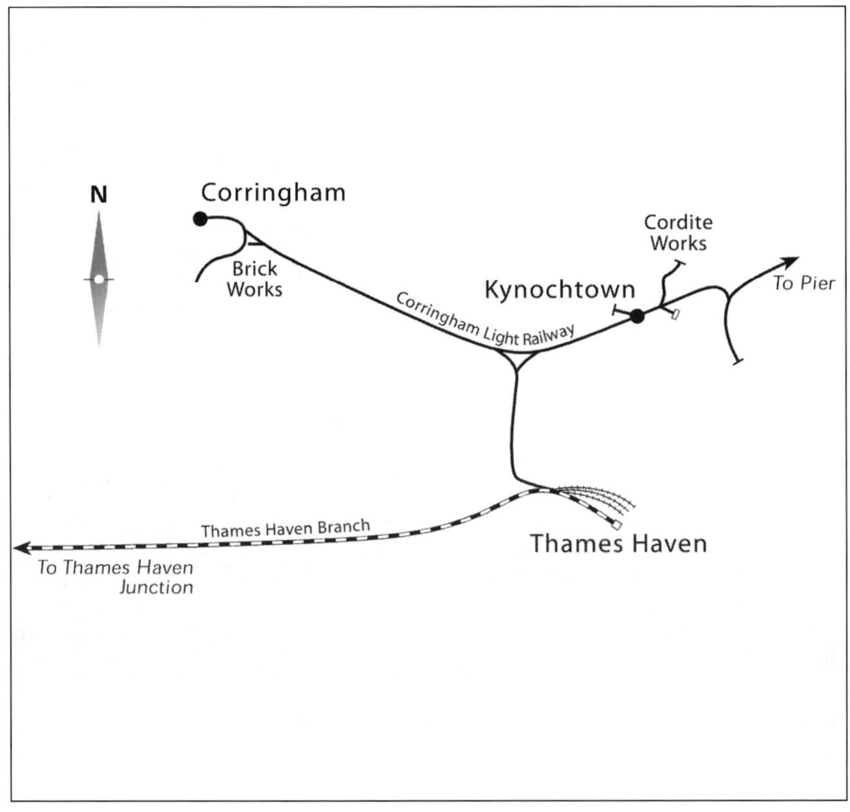

The Corringham Light Railway

Like the Elsenham & Thaxted Railway, the 2¾ mile line between Corringham and Kynochtown (Coryton) on the north bank of the Thames was built under the provisions of the 1896 Light Railways Act. However, unlike the North Woolwich branch further upstream, it had no intention of opening up the marshy wastes over which it ran to farming or settlement, for its sole aim was to serve an explosives factory.

The Birmingham firm of G. Kynoch & Company Ltd had picked a remote Essex marshland site in 1896 for the factory, as it would be well away from any centre of population should the worst happen. The company bought land at Borley Farm next to Shellhaven Creek in 1895 and built the factory there two years later. However, they needed to bring its 600-strong workforce in and out on a daily basis.

The line ran from Corringham to Shellhaven, with a separate branch to the workers' settlement of Kynochtown. It was opened for freight on 1 January 1901 and to passengers on 22 June that year. The little line was also

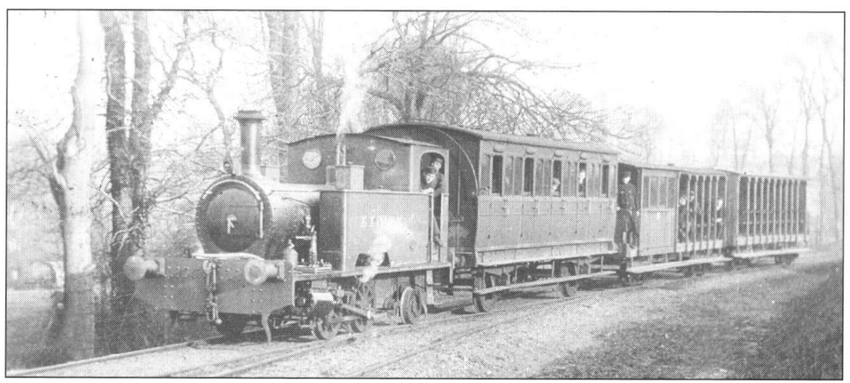

A typical passenger train on the Corringham Light Railway. (Nigel Bowdidge collection)

linked to the London Tilbury & Southend Railway's Thames Haven branch from Thames Haven Junction near Stanford-le-Hope through a siding connection. The passenger station which was built at Thames Haven closed before the Corringham Light Railway opened (see below).

By law, the light railway was a separate concern from Kynoch, but nonetheless was still owned and run by the company. The London Tilbury & Southend had a statutory provision to take over the light railway, but never exercised it.

Six passenger trains a day made the 12-minute journey, and as it was legally a public service rather than a totally private concern just for the explosives factory, some workers at the nearby Shell petrol plant also used it. Incidentally, there is no historical connection between the local topographical name Shellhaven (later Shell Haven) and the Shell petroleum conglomerate which dates from the 1890s, although there was an Oil Mill Farm in the vicinity since the early 1800s.

A Corringham Light Railway train at the line's northern terminus in its early years. (Andrew Neale collection)

Not only was the line one of the shortest public railways in Britain, but unusually it was operated without the use of signals. The light railway also carried coal for public use, and was linked to a brickworks at Corringham, as well as other goods traffic, via Thames Haven, although the coal for the Kynoch works arrived by sea. Most of the manufactured ammunition was taken out by barge to Woolwich Arsenal on the far side of the Thames.

As might be expected, the Corringham Light Railway had its heyday in the First World War when coal had to be brought in by rail and demands for ammunition production were so great that two more engines and ten bogie carriages were bought. In all, its fleet had five tank engines, and they were also used for shunting within the Kynoch works.

After the war, Kynoch merged with Eley-Nobel Ltd, which sold on the business to coal and oil fuel suppliers Cory Brothers Ltd of Cardiff. The explosive works closed in 1919 but the light railway survived as a separate entity. Cory Brothers took over the railway and renamed Kynochtown as Coryton. In 1923 the firm built oil storage tanks along with a small refinery next to the site of the explosives works. The company produced a well-known brand of petrol, Corey's Motor Spirit.

By 1930, passenger numbers on the light railway had dropped to 30 a day, primarily because the Manorway road across the marshes had been upgraded to take cars and buses. However, the railway again experienced a boom time after war broke out in 1939, while the refineries and oil storage tanks at Thames Haven, Shell Haven and Coryton became a prime Luftwaffe target, notably in September 1940 during the Battle of Britain. Shortly before D-Day in 1944, the line was used to move vast amounts of war supplies which had been stored in the area.

The passenger service was restored on 8 November 1945, but by this time many workers travelled by bus and the rail traffic largely consisted of enthusiast specials. In 1950, the line was taken over by the Vacuum Oil Company, later known as Mobil, which eventually replaced the steam engines with diesel locomotives.

The light railway's passenger trains continued until 1952, although by then they had lost the battle against rival bus services. The line to Corringham was lifted that year, leaving only the section between Coryton and Thames Haven, which was then upgraded to main-line standard. The last of the light railway locomotives were cut up on site in 1957, and although the line had physically gone, the operating company still existed in law until it was transferred to Mobil in 1969.

A new refinery began operating in 1953. In the seventies, with the last residents moving out to places like Basildon, Coryton village was demolished and the land that it had occupied became absorbed into the refinery site, which is still connected to the national rail network via the freight-only Thames Haven branch. Indeed, the old Coryton platform from the post-Kynochtown light railway days is, surprisingly, still in place on the freight-only branch, complete with its nameboard.

The Thames Haven branch

Of all the public, as opposed to the private industrial railways in Essex, the Thames Haven branch from Stanford-le-Hope probably remains the least known. Although it was for a long time a freight-only branch serving the oil terminals at Thames Haven and Coryton, it did carry passengers in its very early days, and as such it is a lost route that concerns us here.

The origins of the line go back to 1836, when Parliament passed an Act authorising its construction by the Thames

Haven Dock & Railway Company. The far-sighted promoters saw the benefits of a deepwater dock for London if a railway could be built to link it to the capital. Construction work began in March 1854, after a fresh Act was obtained in the year before following years of deliberations.

Running from Thames Haven Junction on the London, Tilbury & Southend Railway, the line was three miles and 67 chains long, and led to a new port immediately to the west of Shell Haven, to be known as Thames Haven. It opened on 7 June 1855, in time for that summer's Thames passenger steamer services to Margate to call there. Steamers took 2½ hours for the trip from Thames Haven to Margate. However, Thames Haven offered only a slight advantage over Tilbury in terms of the time needed for the trip.

The Thames steamer services were badly hit after the sinking of a vessel on 3 September 1878, when around 700 people were drowned after the *Princess Alice* was involved in a collision. The disaster in itself had nothing to do with Thames Haven, but the railway management, which had already expressed concerns about the failure of the Margate steamer passenger trade to grow as expected, ended the ships' calls to the pier at the end of the 1880 season.

One very unusual event took place at Thames Haven station on 26 November 1862, in the form of an illegal bare-fist prize fight. The sport may have been outlawed but it still had wide support and continued until it was suppressed in the later 1860s. Because local police forces broke up the fights, the venues were announced to supporters only at the last minute, and some railway companies were prepared to run special trains in conjunction with them, including the Eastern Counties Railway. Venues were chosen for their remoteness, and the estuary marshes were therefore considered ideal. This particular event at the station featured bouts between Tom King and Jem Mace, and Hicks and Gallagher, the latter being stopped by the intervention of Rainham and Grays police. The contestants and spectators merely boarded a waiting steamer and went across to Kent where they carried on the fight.

Public passenger services on the Thames Haven branch ceased after the Margate steamers stopped calling, although in 1881 special trains were run to bring in labourers from East London to mend a breach in the sea wall at Thames Haven. Also, specials were run in 1910 and 1912 to bring in managers of the London & Thames Haven Oil Wharves Company and the branch went on to thrive as a goods line, firstly with cattle and sheep, and then with oil, petroleum and explosives. A new service for workmen from Tilbury and East Tilbury to Thames Haven began on 1 January 1923.

Four intermediate and very basic halts – merely surfaced areas with small shelters – were provided at Mayes Crossing, Curry Marsh, London & Thames Haven Oil Wharves and Thames Haven. The first rake of coaches comprised 17 old four-wheel carriages. The service lasted until 9 June 1958.

While closed to public passengers, Thames Haven station remained open to the public for goods. The original station of 1855 was demolished in 1954, a year after a replacement building was provided at nearby Dock House level crossing.

The Thames Haven line is still operational for freight. A proposal by shipping line P&O for redevelopment of the adjacent closed Shell refinery as a major part of the London Gateway deep water container port project received Government approval in May 2007 despite local opposition. Thames Haven, Shell Haven, Coryton and the freight branch which serves them have clearly not seen the last of transport developments.

Tilbury Riverside

Just as the North Woolwich branch on the north side of the river Thames was built to serve a town on the south bank, so Tilbury Riverside station was planned to link to Kent, again via a ferry service. The London Tilbury & Southend Railway, promoted by the Eastern Counties Railway and the London & Blackwall Railway by a Parliamentary Act of 1852, built a short spur at Tilbury along with a pier. The aim was to offer passengers cheap travel from Fenchurch Street to Gravesend.

A triangular junction was built between Tilbury Town and East Tilbury leading to the station which was originally known as Tilbury Fort when it opened on 13 April 1854. The 'Fort' suffix was discarded shortly afterwards. Travelling to Southend, most trains from Tilbury Town would reverse at the station and then carry on to East Tilbury.

The ferry linked the pier to Gravesend Town Pier, directly competing with the South Eastern Railway which had reached Gravesend five years earlier. As at North Woolwich, the Tilbury pier also served steamers plying their trade in the Thames estuary.

In 1881, the London Tilbury & Southend Railway came up with a proposal to replace the ferry with a tunnel linking its line to the London, Chatham & Dover Railway at Gravesend. However, the eyes of the London Tilbury & Southend Railway were here too big for its belly, and as it was short of money, the tunnel was never built.

The LT&SR became part of the Midland Railway in 1912. In turn, the Midland was absorbed into the London Midland & Scottish Railway (LMS) at the Grouping on 1 January 1923.

The Port of London Authority and the LMS built a floating landing stage which was officially opened by Britain's first Labour Prime Minister, Ramsay McDonald.

Class 302 electric multiple unit No 243 departs from Tilbury Riverside after reversal, forming the 10.35 am service from Fenchurch Street to Shoeburyness on 17 January 1981. (Brian Morrison)

The landing stage allowed liners to berth at all states of the tide, and opened up major new potential for boat-train traffic.

The LMS renamed the station Tilbury Riverside on 6 July 1936. However, growing car ownership led to a decline in its importance as a passenger ferry terminal, and the opening of the Dartford Tunnel in 1963 resulted in major cutbacks in services to Riverside. Goods traffic ended on 6 May 1968, and the passenger services were finally withdrawn by train operator Network SouthEast on 28 November 1992. The ferry still runs, and is nowadays operated by a private company, with the pier being accessed only via a shuttle bus from Tilbury Town.

The Riverside station building survives in use as the Tilbury Riverside Arts Activity Centre, but the platforms and carriage sidings have gone. However, the triangular

Class 302 EMUs Nos 240, 290, 299 and 248 in Tilbury Riverside sidings on 17 January 1981. (Brian Morrison)

junction which brought trains to Riverside is still there, serving Tilbury's container terminal.

Samuel Williams' wharves lines

The many wharves and industrial concerns on the north bank of the river Thames in Essex spawned a variety of internal railway systems, in addition to the Port of London Authority and Beckton Gas Works systems already mentioned. Two of the biggest of these lines have each bequeathed us a steam locomotive for posterity, albeit in exile from Essex.

Dagenham has for more than a century been a centre of heavy industry, and is best known for its Ford motor car plant, which has for a long time had its own internal railway system and locomotive fleet. However, it was local industrialist Samuel Williams who transformed the town from a fishing port to a vibrant manufacturing centre, by turning the riverfront into a major dock in 1887.

A scheme for a dock at Dagenham linked by railway to the main line at Chadwell Heath had been proposed in 1846, and although a pier was built in 1865, no further development took place until the arrival of Williams, a lighterman from Lambeth. Until then, the only industry of note was a small munitions factory and a candlemaking works.

At Dagenham, Williams expanded into civil engineering, barge building, ship owning and fuel trading. Two new jetties were built to form a tidal basin with a quay. Other firms were drawn to the area by Williams' new facilities, and Dagenham Marsh became an area of heavy industry, with engineering, chemical and paint factories.

Samuel Williams & Sons built a new deep-water jetty in 1903, the first concrete structure of its kind on the river. It was designed to carry railway tracks and heavy lifting gear so that colliers could unload cargoes there at any state of the tide.

Manning Wardle 0-6-0 saddle tank Sharpthorne, *part of the Samuel Williams & Sons fleet, and seen in its days on the firm's internal system, is now preserved at the Bluebell Railway in Sussex, which as a contractor's locomotive it helped build. (Andrew Neale collection)*

The firm eventually owned the entire riverfront from Horseshoe Corner to the river Beam and northwards to the London, Tilbury & Southend Railway. Williams built Dagenham Dock station in conjunction with the railway company in 1908, and a substantial internal railway system, laid to standard gauge, grew to serve the flourishing wharves. The Ford Motor Company bought land from the Williams family in 1924 and built a factory on reclaimed marshes which began turning out motor cars in October 1931.

Samuel Williams & Sons closed in 1985. Today the best-known of its substantial locomotive fleet is perhaps the 1877-built Manning Wardle 0-6-0 saddle tank *Sharpthorne*. It was previously owned by contractor Joseph Firbank, who built the Lewes & East Grinstead Railway (the locomotive took its name from a nearby Sussex village), but from 1888 until 1982 it belonged to Samuel Williams & Sons and was used on the firm's Dagenham coal dock until being withdrawn in 1958. It escaped the scrapman to become one of the first locomotives to be privately preserved, and after being loaned to Bressingham Steam Museum at Diss in Norfolk, it returned to the line that it had helped build, the Bluebell Railway, for its centenary celebrations in 1982.

When Samuel Williams & Sons went out of business, the little engine was bought by the Bluebell from the receivers because of its historical links. However, it is not big enough to haul passenger trains, and, as its overhaul to running order is not considered a priority, for many years it has been left on static display outside Sheffield Park station.

Chalk and cement

Large chalk deposits which appear as cliffs at Purfleet have been a source of industry since medieval times. Chalk was used for making lime and bricks as well as agricultural fertiliser. In early times, chalk was dug out in primitive pits called deneholes, several of which survive at Purfleet.

The industry later took off because the north bank of the Thames was suitable for wharves and jetties to be built, allowing easy export of the products to London. In 1794, Samuel Whitbread, who was the landlord of several Purfleet chalk quarries, took steps to mechanise them, and introduced horse-drawn tramways which preceded the development of the steam engine.

By 1839 there were around 85 chalk pits in the parish, but with changes in agricultural practices, they fell into sharp decline and were all closed by 1850. However, the increasing use of cement in the mid-19th century saw many quarries reopened and new ones dug. Inevitably, several of them used railways in some form or another.

Purfleet has been the home of Flora, Bertolli and Stork margarine for the best part of a century. The former Van den Berghs & Jurgens margarine works, now Unilever, was said to be the largest in the world. It was set up in 1917, and had its own internal railway system, using fireless locomotives to prevent the spread of sparks from steam. Barclay 0-4-0 fireless locomotive No 1493 of 1916 is seen in the works on 25 April 1959. (53A Models of Hull collection)

Merchant's son Henry Brown, a London bank clerk who made a small fortune from trading and mining during five years in Australia's Victoria gold fields, established the Northfleet Coal and Ballast Company on the Thames estuary in Kent in the 1870s. When this quarry became exhausted in 1895, the company moved to the far side of the river and set up the Thurrock Chalk & Whiting Company in Essex, which continued its operations until 1973. The company eventually became a subsidiary of Associated Portland Cement Manufacturers, which is now part of the Blue Circle Group.

Operations at Thurrock expanded, and new quarries were opened up near London Road. The company laid its own standard-gauge light railway with an extensive fleet of locomotives hauling trucks from the quarry half a mile to the works, and then on to the jetties on the Thames estuary for shipment to North America and elsewhere. The line not only had a transhipment siding with the London, Tilbury & Southend Railway but crossed it via a bridge on the way to the wharves beyond West Thurrock marshes. The system used antiquated Victorian side-tipping wagons right into the sixties, and they are believed to have been the last of their type to operate in Britain.

When the Lafarge Aluminous Cement Company Limited was set up in 1925 on the site of an exhausted quarry, Thurrock Chalk & Whiting took the opportunity to provide rail services to it. The company's system was expanded again in 1938 when the Thurrock Flint Company was established, flints being a by-product of chalk quarrying.

When the Alpha Cement Works was established next to the Lafarge works just before the Second World War, a railway was laid to link it to another new quarry, with Thurrock Chalk & Whiting building and operating it. After the war, Alpha brought in locomotives of its own. The Thurrock Chalk & Whiting system was dieselised in 1966, with new side-tipping coal wagons bought, but it closed altogether in the mid-seventies. The plant is now part of the Lafarge operation.

One of the Thurrock Chalk & Whiting locomotives, 0-4-0 saddle tank *Swanscombe*, the oldest surviving Andrew Barclay locomotive in the United Kingdom, was delivered new to the Northfleet Coal and Ballast Company in 1891 before being transferred to new quarries and wharves at West Thurrock in Essex, which had been opened in 1912-13, around a decade after Henry Brown's death. *Swanscombe* was eventually deemed unsuitable for the heavier loads hauled on the heavy-graded line from the chalk quarry to the Thames jetties, and was relegated to shunting duties.

Given a new boiler in 1929, and a new firebox in 1941, *Swanscombe* was bought by a member of the Quainton Railway Society in 1965, an enthusiast group, and is now

Andrew Barclay 0-4-0 saddle tank Swanscombe, *pictured at work on the Thurrock Chalk & Whiting system in April 1936. (Keith Lobley collection)*

preserved at the Buckinghamshire Railway Centre at Quainton Road station north of Aylesbury. The engine was restored and was steamed in 1975 for the BBC *Play School* programme, where it became a popular character. After many years out of service, *Swanscombe* was again returned to traffic at the Centre in 2002.

Tunnel Portland Cement, which was adjacent to Thurrock Whiting, also had its own rail system. It was about a mile long, with main-line sidings, and a steam fleet which comprised around eight saddle tanks, exclusively built by Peckett. Dating from 1874, its cement works were acquired by the Danish company F.L. Smidth in 1911 and were rebuilt, and by 1968 it was the biggest in western Europe, with 1,200 staff. The Tunnel cement railway system closed around 1967/68.

At Grays, there were two cement works railways. The system at the Blue Circle cement works dated from around 1900, and also used a fleet of Peckett saddle tanks, until the firm replaced its railway with a conveyor belt in 1960. The Grays Chalk Quarries Company, however, was set up around 1850 when it became one of the first industrial operations in south-east England to use steam locomotives. At one stage its mile-long line had a fleet of about 12 locomotives, but it closed as early as 1951.

The Thames marshes tip railways

For much of the 20th century, coal was shipped up the Thames to supply London, and the capital's domestic waste was loaded into the empty barges that returned downstream. The waste was offloaded on wharves at Rainham and Purfleet and taken in side-tipping railway trucks along basic tracks to rubbish tips, infilling what were deemed to be 'useless' marshes on the north bank of the

Swanscombe, a children's favourite on BBC's Play School, is now preserved at the Buckinghamshire Railway Centre. (BRC)

Peckett 0-4-0 saddle tank No 1806 of 1930 Fola hard at work on the Tunnel Portland Cement works system at Thurrock in 1959. (53A Models of Hull collection)

Thames, in the days before the country became more ecologically aware.

Five standard-gauge railways were laid for this purpose, each about half a mile long, and using very small 0-4-0 saddle tanks as motive power. Three were operated by William Cory, one by H. Covington & Son and one by W.R. Cunice. Dating from the turn of the century, most closed in the 1950s, but the Cunice line was still running at Rainham in the early 1970s.

The tracks were of a temporary nature, so they could be moved around once particular sites were full up. None of the locomotives have survived. It is believed that this type of railway was unique in Britain to Essex and the Thames marshes.

5
Following Colne and Stour

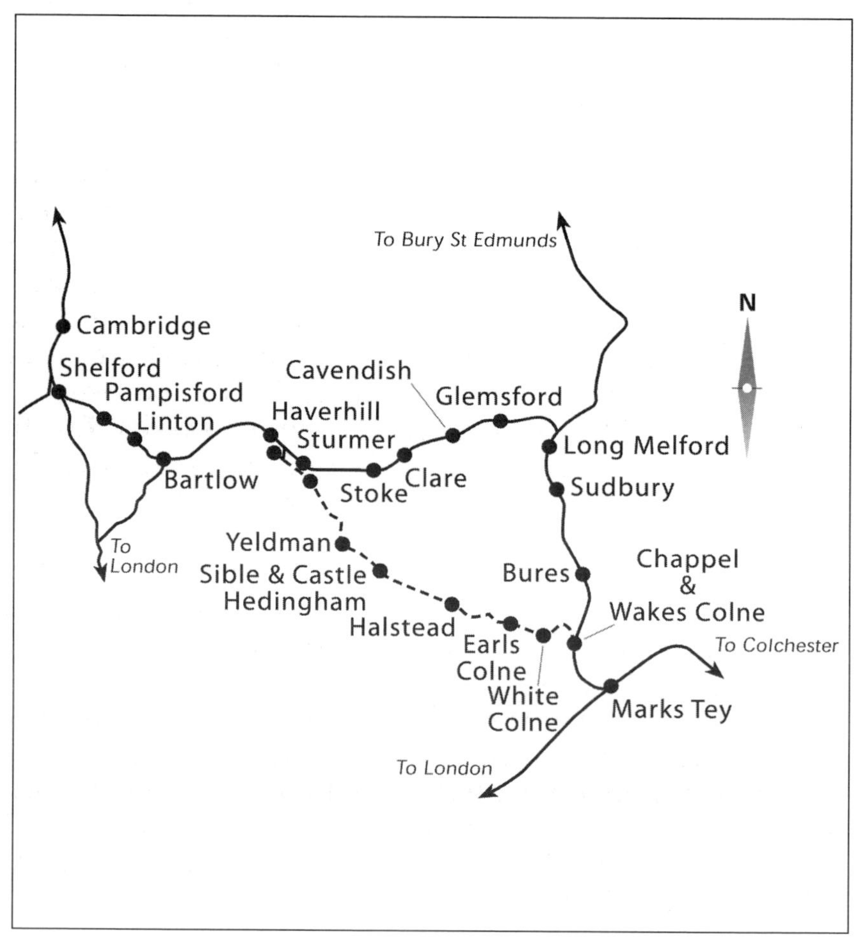

The Stour Valley Railway

One of the longest west to east cross-country routes which served East Anglia, the Stour Valley line which ran from Cambridge to Marks Tey via Long Melford was not only a backbone of many smaller branch lines and byways, taking goods to isolated communities, but carried much holiday traffic in the summer months. It hugged the boundary between Essex and Suffolk for much of its length, crossing from one county to another at regular intervals, and took nearly two decades to complete throughout.

The Eastern Counties Railway to Colchester in 1843 had bypassed Sudbury, leaving it 11 miles to the north. The Colchester, Stour Valley, Sudbury & Halstead Railway received parliamentary authority to construct a 12-mile line between Marks Tey and Sudbury in 1846, and in June the following year, further acts were obtained for an extension from Sudbury to Clare with a branch from Melford to Bury St Edmunds. The company was leased to the Ipswich & Bury St Edmunds Railway which in turn leased the Stour Valley undertaking to the Eastern Union Railway in November 1848. The first section, from Marks Tey to Sudbury, was opened on 2 July 1849 and was taken over by the Eastern Counties Railway on 7 August 1862.

The greatest physical barrier encountered by the builders was the valley of the river Colne at Chappel, where the magnificent 1,066 ft viaduct was built to cross it. It was originally intended to build a wooden viaduct, but by chance, the workmen discovered brick earth on the site. With a ready source of raw materials so close at hand, the viaduct was built from bricks instead. However, the soil was so hard that gunpowder had to be used to shift it in places. Around seven million bricks were needed to build the 32 arches, each with a 30 ft span, and 606 men and 106 horses toiled to finish the job.

Playing to the Whistle *is the title of this portrait of Halstead in the fifties by acclaimed tr*
goods', passes the home of Halstead Town FC, who today are members of the Ridgeons Ea

painter Malcolm Root, who lives locally. A J15 0-6-0, colloquially known as a 'little black ootball League. (Reproduced with kind permission of Malcolm Root)

Long Melford signal box, with Bernard Salter in charge. (Foxearth Historical Society)

Great Eastern Railway Class C12 4-4-2 tank engine No 67385 nears Long Melford with its passenger train on 24 August 1953. (L.R. Peters)

The project's chief engineer, Peter Bruff, later gave a talk to the Institute of Civil Engineers, with Isambard Kingdom Brunel, the founder of the Great Western Railway and one of the world's greatest engineers, in the audience.

Beyond Bures, the construction team had to tackle the steep Mount Bures ridge, digging two miles of deep cuttings before the line dipped at a 1-in-80 gradient towards Bures, where the Thatchers Arms pub was opened specifically for the labourers.

The dangers of not treating a steam locomotive with loving care and 100 per cent attention were highlighted by an accident on the evening of 25 November 1858, when a train was leaving Bures for Marks Tey. The locomotive boiler exploded and lumps of metals were hurled up to 100 yards away. While the footplate crew miraculously escaped uninjured, doors in the village were blown open by the force of the blast.

The viaduct which linked the Colne Valley & Halstead line through Haverhill to the town's northern station and the Shelford to Sudbury route. (Author)

There were four trains each way on weekdays between Marks Tey and Sudbury in 1850, one of which carried on to Colchester.

In July 1860, the Sudbury & Clare Railway Company revived the 1847 act for the route, and obtained fresh powers to build the line. However, it was taken over by the Eastern Counties Railway which had a wider objective, the building of a new through route from Sudbury to Shelford on the London-Cambridge main line, plus the branch from Long Melford to Bury St Edmunds.

The Great Eastern Railway, successor to the Eastern Counties Railway, opened the line from Shelford to Haverhill on 1 June 1865, extending it to Sudbury on 9 August that year. The branch from Bury St Edmunds was also completed. The Cambridge to Marks Tey line was connected to the Colne Valley and Halstead Railway at both Haverhill and Chappel & Wakes Colne.

When services started between Cambridge, Shelford and Haverhill, three trains each way ran on weekdays. The

A Marks Tey to Cambridge train behind a Holden E4 tender locomotive, leaves Cavendish in 1951 heading towards Clare alongside Stour Street. (Foxearth Historical Society)

A Holden 2-4-0 tender engine sets off from Cavendish station in Great Eastern days with a five-coach train behind it. (Foxearth Historical Society)

One of the LNER's B17 'Footballer' class of 4-6-0 tender engines, No 61651 Derby County, departs from Haverhill on 5 July 1952. (L.R Peters)

frequency was extended to six passenger trains each way by the 1890s, mostly running from Cambridge or Bury St Edmunds to Marks Tey or Colchester. Coal traffic between Peterborough and Colchester and agricultural produce comprised most of the freight carried by the route.

The period before the First World War saw regular through trains between Cambridge and Clacton via Sudbury. However, the decline in rail use caused by increased competition from road transport had set in. The Second World War gave the route a new lease of life, with airfields being established throughout the area. After hostilities ended, through excursion trains returned once again to Clacton and Walton-on-the-Naze. In summer 1954, a regular express ran in each direction on Saturdays between Leicester, Cambridge, Sudbury and Clacton, hauled by the famous B17 Sandringham class 4-6-0

A Sunday excursion to Clacton-on-Sea headed by Ivatt 2MT 2-6-0 No 46467 pictured between Halstead and Earls Colne on 3 August 1959. (Berwyn Stevens/Malcolm Root collection)

locomotives. Interestingly, the old Great Eastern Railway blue station nameboards continued to be used until the 1950s, when they were replaced by the British Railway versions. Many Great Eastern locomotives and carriages also continued in service, long after they had been declared obsolete on far busier routes.

Steam gave way to diesel multiple units and railcars on 1 January 1959, making considerable savings, but despite a brief upturn in passenger numbers, it did little overall to stop people switching from rail to road, as was happening all over the country. Locomotives in the form of Class 31 diesels operated occasional Leicester to Clacton-on-Sea excursions. Cutbacks bit hard in the early sixties, with conductor guards being introduced to collect fares on board trains while all stations became unstaffed apart from Haverhill and Sudbury.

A rare view of a North British diesel electric Type 2 locomotive heading through Halstead with a mixed goods train on 16 April 1960. One of the first generation of diesels to replace steam locomotives on the national network, this type proved unpopular and was withdrawn by the early 1970s. (Berwyn Stevens/Malcolm Root collection)

Passenger trains on the associated route from Long Melford to Bury St Edmunds ended on 10 April 1961, with Bures, Cavendish and Bartlow stations on the main route from Cambridge to Marks Tey closed to freight on 28 December 1964.

The twilight years saw two trains a day run between Sudbury and Cambridge, four between Colchester and Cambridge and six between Marks Tey or Colchester and Sudbury, with the same number making return trips. Most services were operated by diesel multiple units.

In April 1965, the British Railways Board applied for permission to end passenger services from the whole route between Marks Tey and Cambridge. The move promoted local outrage, and as was so often the case elsewhere, any protests by residents seemed doomed to failure, despite local councils showing some willingness to offer a subsidy before the high costs became apparent. All freight services

Bartlow station, near the junction with the Saffron Walden line, has now been converted into a private house called The Booking Hall. *(Author)*

An unidentified 0-4-4 tank pauses at Bartlow with a short rake of vintage coaches. (L.R. Peters collection)

The last-ever passenger train crosses the level crossing at Cavendish on 6 March 1967. (Foxearth Historical Society)

on the Stour Valley line were withdrawn on 31 October 1966, and passenger services between Sudbury and Cambridge ended on 6 March 1967, the track being lifted by demolition contractor A. King and Sons of Norwich in 1970.

However, the protesters scored a partial and major victory in managing to keep the section between Sudbury and Marks Tey open, because of the fact that Sudbury was expanding and there was a potential growth in commuter traffic. Sadly, there was no reprieve for the Sudbury to Cambridge section. Further attempts were made to close the Marks Tey to Sudbury section, but it was given an indefinite reprieve after the 1974 energy crisis which led to the threat of petrol rationing, and has survived to this day.

In 1995, the Cambridge to Sudbury Rail Renewal Association was formed to campaign for the reinstatement of the line. Subsequent petitions in Cambridge, Haverhill, Clare, Long Melford and Sudbury were signed by more than

Sturmer station, just inside the Essex boundary, also survives as a private house. (Author)

At Clare station, now the centre of the Clare Castle Country Park, a short length of rail runs into the goods shed. Outside, the crane has been kept as another reminder of times past. In 2004, enthusiasts used a preserved British Railways Scammell 'mechanical horse' to set up a cameo scene from the steam age, beneath the ruins of the medieval castle. (Geoff Silcock)

11,000 people, and a feasibility study indicated that nearly three out of four people questioned would use the route if it was reopened.

The East Anglian Railway Museum

It was not only angry local residents who tried to save the Cambridge to Sudbury route. An enthusiast-led group, the

The booking office and waiting room at Clare station have also survived. (Author)

The final passenger train on the Cambridge to Sudbury line leaves Glemsford station. There have been repeated calls for the route to be rebuilt. (Foxearth Historical Society)

Stour Valley Railway Preservation Society was formed on 24 September 1968 with the very over-ambitious aim of preserving all of the Sudbury to Shelford line. The group's aspirations were soon whittled down to just the three miles from Sudbury to Long Melford, but even this proved beyond its grasp, as the funds to buy the section could not be raised.

In December 1969, the group established a headquarters at Chappel & Wakes Colne station on the Marks Tey to Sudbury section which was still open. British Rail gave the group a lease on the redundant goods yard, goods shed, signal box and station buildings, a site which by then was largely derelict.

The first public steaming took place less than four months after the group moved in, but the only operational locomotive was a Hunslet 0-6-0 industrial saddle tank named *Gunby*. It carried passengers in a contractor's weighing van over a third of a mile of relaid track. Other locomotives and stock followed, while the group set about restoring the buildings.

Operations at the site would always be limited to the track in the goods yard and within the station limits alongside one platform, but at the time, many people believed that the Marks Tey to Sudbury line would soon be closed – and if that happened, the preservationists may have built up sufficient resources to take it over and operate it from their Chappel base.

The group brought a redundant footbridge from Sudbury, bought land on which to build an engine restoration shed and workshop, and rescued and re-erected the Grade I listed signal box from Mistley on the Harwich branch, after buying it for just £5. The society's limited company was successful in buying the whole site from British Rail at auction in 1987, after selling a locomotive to a group of members.

Possibly the first time that a J15 0-6-0 has been seen at Platform 2 of Chappel & Wakes Colne station, since the late fifties, was when sole survivor No 65462 visited for an enthusiasts' photographic event on 23 September 2004. (Geoff Silcock)

With the resurgence in use of the Sudbury branch, as the remaining stub of the cross-country route had become, the society changed direction. Realising it had amassed a sizeable collection of rolling stock and artefacts from the region's lines, the site was repackaged in 1986 as the East Anglian Railway Museum.

It was three years later that the society's flagship locomotive, Great Eastern Railway N7 class 0-6-2 tank engine No 69621, the sole survivor of a type that had once been seen on many now-lost branch lines in Essex, returned to steam.

In 1991, the society obtained a Light Railway Order to allow the running of trains, and in 1999, major celebrations were staged to mark the 150th anniversary of the opening of the Colchester, Sudbury, Stour Valley and Halstead Railway, at the same time as the Sudbury to Marks Tey route was repackaged as the Gainsborough Line (the great portrait and landscape painter Thomas Gainsborough, 1727–1788, was born in Sudbury). The museum provided a re-enactment of the opening train with guests in period clothes and a brass band.

If ever the Sudbury branch is declared surplus to requirements, there will be those ready to step in and prevent it from joining the other lost lines in this book.

Incidentally, *Gunby*, the little 1941-built engine that started it all, is now at the Swindon & Cricklade Railway in Wiltshire awaiting restoration.

The Colne Valley & Halstead Railway

Closely associated with the Stour Valley line is the Colne Valley & Halstead Railway, which also connected Chappel to Haverhill, but cut Sudbury off in favour of Halstead. It was planned as a knock-on effect of the line from Marks Tey to Sudbury being built.

The five-miles-and-five-furlongs-long line from the Eastern Counties Railway at Chappel to Halstead was authorised by an Act of Parliament on 30 June 1856. However, the company found it difficult to raise the finance, and it was more than two years before work started.

A dispute with the Eastern Counties Railway arose regarding the siting of the junction at Chappel, and the Colne Valley & Halstead Railway threatened to build its own station nearby. However, all was settled amicably, and the line to Halstead opened on 16 April 1860 – by which time the railway company had been authorised to build a 13-mile extension to Haverhill. Work on the extension began on 19 June 1860, and it was opened in stages. Sible & Castle Hedingham was reached on 1 July 1861, Yeldham on 26 May 1862 and the terminus of Haverhill on 10 May 1863. That year, an extra station was added at Birdbrook.

When the Great Eastern Railway was formed in 1862, the Colne Valley & Halstead Railway remained independent. Three years later, the Great Eastern's Stour Valley route from Sudbury to Cambridge was opened via Haverhill, where a link line joined it to the Colne Valley & Halstead Railway via a massive brick viaduct that still stands today.

Typical of so many lines serving rural backwaters, the Colne Valley & Halstead Railway struggled financially from its opening. It went into receivership in 1874, but fresh finance was raised to buy three engines in 1876. Its most

Great Eastern Railway N7 class 0-6-2 tank engine No 69651 hauls a regular service through Haverhill, where passengers changed for the Colne Valley & Halstead line. (Author's collection).

profitable period came at the turn of the century, before the motor car arrived.

Built to a lighter standard than the Stour Valley line, its services were hauled by tank engines and smaller tender locomotives. The company's stock was serviced at the Great Eastern Railway's Stratford workshops.

The railway stayed independent until it was swallowed up into the London & North Eastern Railway at the Grouping of 1923. At that time, the company had five tank engines of its own, the first, an 0-4-2, built by Neilson of Glasgow and numbered 1, being built in 1887.

The following year, the first cutback was made, when the original Colne Valley & Halstead Railway terminus station at Haverhill lost its passenger service on 14 July in favour of the Great Eastern one via the connecting spur. The original Haverhill station, however, stayed open for goods and was renamed Haverhill South on 1 February 1925, remaining in use until 19 April 1965. As with the Stour Valley line, the Second World War brought an upsurge in traffic, due to several United States Air Force bases opening nearby.

Diesel multiple units were also introduced in 1959, but any savings that they made could only delay the inevitable. Years of steady decline saw the passenger service withdrawn on 30 December 1961, when the line north of Yeldham closed completely, with freight retreating in stages over the rest of the line until 19 April 1965. Demolition crews lifted the track the following year.

However, the line, or at least part of it, would not stay silent. In 1973, two enthusiasts, Dick Hymas and Gordon Warren, walked the old line and came up with plans to relay a section of it and run steam trains as a tourist attraction. Permission was eventually obtained to lay a mile of track to the west of Castle Hedingham, between mileposts 60 and 61 of the original line.

The first preserved steam locomotive, War Department

The gatehouse at the Parsonage Street level crossing in Halstead, pictured after the line's closure, survives today, although the rails have long since gone. (Richard Root)

Austerity 0-6-0 saddle tank No 190, arrived on the line in August 1973. It was brought on the back of a low loader in steam – and as the lorry passed through Hedingham, the whistle was sounded along the main street to show that the railway had returned to this idyllic part of Essex.

The Colne Valley Railway Preservation Society was formed the following year, when a 'new' station, Castle Hedingham, was built on a green field site. The original Sible & Castle Hedingham station (opened as Castle Hedingham) was derelict and awaiting demolition, but the owner agreed to donate it to the society on condition it was taken down within six weeks. It took two years to rebuild brick by brick, but although it has been spirited away to a nearby site which never had a station, its external appearance now is as when it was built in 1861.

Half a mile of spare track and five points lying unused at

Sudbury station were bought from British Rail, while Essex County Council donated the crossing keeper's hut from the former station at White Colne, it becoming a permanent way hut on the revived railway.

That first locomotive, which had been built by Hunslet in 1952, was typical of a design which was mass produced during and after the Second World War for both military and industrial service, some finding their way into the LNER fleet where they became the J94 class. At Easter 1975, it joined another steam engine which had been moved to the new Colne Valley Railway, 1921-built Avonside 0-4-0 saddle tank *Barrington*, in giving footplate rides to visitors. After a public appeal for funds, the society bought its first passenger coach in 1976.

The following year, members searched for more Colne Valley & Halstead Railway original buildings but could find none available, so it was decided to build one from scratch for the second platform at Castle Hedingham. Raw materials were salvaged from station sites along the original line, and the foundations of the old Halstead station were dug up to contribute. A shortfall in authentic bricks was tackled by making new ones by hand to match the reclaimed originals.

The redundant signal box from Cressing on the Braintree to Witham line, which dated from 1898, was acquired from British Rail and re-erected at Castle Hedingham. In 1982, the sole surviving original girder bridge from Earls Colne (originally called Forest Gate) was used to replace the missing one over the river Colne, allowing the heritage line to expand as far as Nunnery Street, to which trains began running in 1986. The run-round loop at Nunnery Street is controlled by a Great Eastern Railway signal box retrieved from Wrabness on the still-extant Manningtree to Harwich line, thereby ensuring the survival of yet another piece of Essex transport heritage.

The Colne Valley Railway in 2004, with visiting J15 0-6-0 No 65462 taking the identity of former Colchester-based sister engine No 65465 for an enthusiasts' charter at Castle Hedingham station. (Geoff Silcock)

Since then, the Colne Valley Railway, although remaining one of Britain's shorter standard-gauge heritage lines, has become a significant tourist attraction and also a restoration base and home for many other preserved locomotives, both steam and diesel. The volunteers who run it boast that the mile-long line carries more passengers each year today than the entire 20-mile railway ever did in its heyday.

6
Mid Essex: from Hertfordshire to the Coast

The Bishop's Stortford, Dunmow & Braintree Railway
Two lines to Maldon: from Witham and from Woodham Ferrers

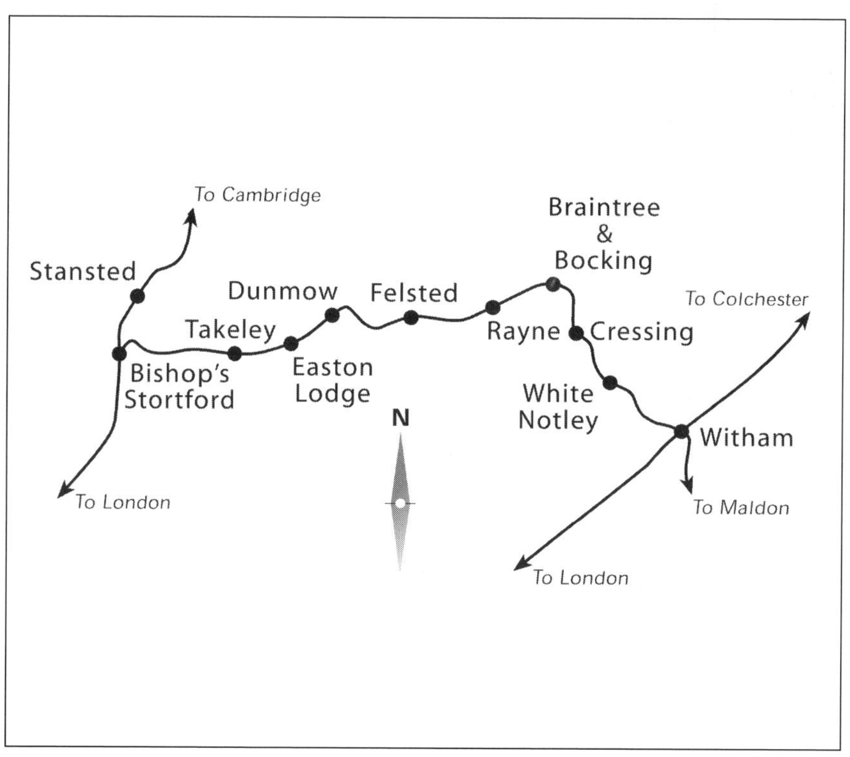

The Bishop's Stortford, Dunmow & Braintree Railway

'Hey – what about us?' was the question being asked in the mid-Essex market town of Dunmow when it became apparent that it was being missed out by the national railway network. The Great Northern Railway had considered building its main line between London and York via Dunmow, before opting for the present route of the East Coast Main Line. Had it chosen otherwise, Dunmow would likely have become another Stevenage or Hatfield, at least in size.

Bishop's Stortford had become rail-connected in 1842 with the opening of the Northern & Eastern line, later to be taken over by the Eastern Counties Railway. Braintree received its link to the network with the opening of the line to Witham and Maldon in 1848. Therefore Dunmow, midway between the pair, was clearly feeling left out.

In the early 1850s, the Bury St Edmunds Railway Company made plans for a route between Bury St Edmunds and London via Dunmow. The scheme was vigorously opposed by the Eastern Counties Railway who were concerned that its monopoly in East Anglia would be threatened, and who, in 1859, persuaded the Epping Railway to obtain an Act of Parliament to extend its line from Chipping Ongar to Dunmow.

A breakthrough came when a group of Hertfordshire businessmen who wanted easy transport for malt and barley from towns and villages in west Essex deposited plans for a railway with Parliament under the name of the Bishop's Stortford, Dunmow & Braintree Railway in 1860/1. The plans included the branch from Dunmow to Chipping Ongar joining the Epping Railway's line, but it was never built. Had it been, Dunmow would again have had a fast route to the capital, and would probably look very different today.

The line was hailed by its promoters as having great potential, being a straight and direct route across north Essex linking Bishop's Stortford, Hertfordshire and the Stort navigations with mid-Essex towns and the coast.

The first turf was ceremonially cut at Dunmow on 24 February 1864, but the company fell into financial difficulties, businessmen in both Bishop's Stortford and Braintree being lukewarm about the whole scheme, and it was left to the GER to promote a bill in 1865 to absorb the line and to raise the share capital needed to complete it.

The 17¾-mile largely single-track route was opened on 22 February 1869 with intermediate stations at Takeley, Felsted and Rayne. Further stops were added – Easton Lodge in 1894, Hockerill Halt in 1910 and Stane Street and

Felsted station on 23 February 1952, with F5 2-4-2T No 67196 hauling a two-coach train in the final week of passenger services. (J.H. Meredith)

A Braintree-bound service heads east from Takeley station. (Lens of Sutton)

Easton Lodge Halt in Great Eastern days, with the crossing keeper's cottage on the right. (Lens of Sutton)

Easton Lodge Halt today; the cottage still stands, as does the wooden hut which housed the levers for operating the gate signals. (Author)

Banister Green halts in 1922. Easton Lodge Halt was built primarily as a private station by the Countess of Warwick, and used by the rich and famous and by royalty. The Prince of Wales, later King Edward VIII, made frequent visits to see the earl and countess at their nearby Easton Lodge home. The countess agreed to pay GER £52 annually for ten years for the upkeep of the halt, and that it should be available for public use.

Hockerill Halt was a small request halt built next to Bishop's Stortford's golf club in Dunmow Road, but was little used by members and was eventually suspended from the timetable.

The high expectations of profits and passenger use for the railway never materialised, but the line received a major boost in the 1880s when the sudden demand for agricultural produce in London combined with new factories being built in Braintree led to a boom in freight.

The London & North Eastern Railway, which took over the Great Eastern at the Grouping of the railways in 1923, pulled out all the stops to encourage more passengers to use the line, doubling the three daily passenger trains to six. However, it was freight which formed the primary source of revenue, with Felsted having a 50-wagon passing loop and shunting spur provided in 1926 to serve a large sugar beet factory.

Great Eastern Railway-design 2-4-2 tank engines such as the F5 class formed the mainstay of motive power. Goods trains were required to include a 20-ton brake van because of the steep gradients on the route. The railway was used to transport thousands of tons of rubble for the construction of Saling airfield near Braintree during the Second World War. After the airfield became operational, the line was used to supply it with bombs under cover of darkness, also taking armaments to the United States Air Force bases at Stansted and Easton Lodge. After D-Day in June 1944, the railway was used by ambulance trains to transport wounded soldiers.

Increased car ownership and competition from bus services saw most passenger trains on the line running almost empty after the war, and services were withdrawn as early as 1 March 1952. A large crowd gathered at Braintree to make the final return trip to Bishop's Stortford. The last train departed at 6.30 pm, with a black wreath placed on its boiler by the stationmaster. Four coaches instead of the usual two carried ten times the number of regular passengers, and the train departed Bishop's Stortford at 8.15 pm to the accompaniment of whistles from locomotives' engines in the goods yard and exploding fog signals placed on the line.

The line remained open for freight, with a special goods service running to Hockerill until 1960. Two years later, a new Geest distribution centre for bananas was opened at

Easton Lodge, and in a freight renaissance for the line, up to 300 tons of fruit was transported to the factory every week for ripening.

Meanwhile, excursion trains to Southend-on-Sea and Clacton-on-Sea continued to use the route, while in 1960 British Railways tested its prototype Road Railer on the branch – an ingenious combination where a road lorry tractor unit coupled up to a container which could run on road or railway tracks.

The Beeching Report of 1963 recorded that Bishop's Stortford handled more than 25,000 tons of freight traffic a year, and so the route was spared – for the time being. However, freight services progressively fell by the wayside, with Felsted closing on 4 May 1964, apart from the sugar beet siding, Rayne on 7 December that year and Takeley on 18 December 1966, when the Felsted to Dunmow section closed completely. Easton Lodge to Dunmow was closed on

Dunmow could have been served by an extension of the Ongar line, but ended up on a lossmaking cross-country route which saw little passenger use. It is seen on 28 March 1955 when it was still open for freight only. (Douglas Thompson)

1 April 1969, Braintree to Felsted on 20 June 1970, and finally Bishop's Stortford to Easton Lodge, on 1 March 1972. A last enthusiast special ran from Bishop's Stortford to Easton Lodge and back on 27 July 1972, with most of the track taken up that autumn.

A mile of track from Bishop's Stortford was left in place, because of the possibility it could form the basis of a new line to Stansted Airport, but another route was chosen for that purpose, and the track was lifted in 1974.

Much of the old trackbed now forms the Flitch Way, a long-distance footpath and cycleway from Braintree station (formerly Braintree & Bocking) to Bishop's Stortford. The Dunmow Flitch dates from 1104 and had a custom whereby any couple who could prove that they had not argued for a year and a day after being married were awarded a flitch of bacon. The custom was mentioned in Chaucer's *Wife of Bath's Tale*.

Restored Takeley station now stands alongside the Flitch Way cyclepath. (Author)

Ironically, while Dunmow people 150 years ago, bacon aside, were unhappy about being bypassed by the national rail network, the old railway route is now covered by the town's A120 dual carriageway bypass.

Rayne station has been restored as a visitor centre for the Flitch Way country park, and is one of several old stations that are still in pristine condition albeit in private ownership, including Takeley, Felsted and the Easton Lodge crossing keeper's cottage. Indeed, for those wishing to explore old railways on foot or by cycle, this is probably the most accessible of all the Essex routes.

Trains have, however, not entirely disappeared from the line. In the back garden of a private house in Bishop's Stortford, which has been extended to include part of the old trackbed, runs the 7¼ in gauge Stortford Railway, a 120-ft-long circular line which operates battery-electric locomotives and a County Donegal Railway-style railcar on the railway, with a miniature version of a Jersey Railway

Rayne station is now the office for the Flitch Way country park. (Author)

The Stortford Railway, a private miniature line, now offers the only services on any part of the route to Braintree. (Paul Bennett)

steam railmotor being the latest addition. Occasional open days are held in aid of All Saints parish church at Hockerill.

Two lines to Maldon: from Witham and from Woodham Ferrers

Maldon, famous for its sea salt, today has a population of 60,743. Local government estimates show that mid-Essex will have another 60,000 people living in the area by 2028, with Maldon taking a fair slice.

The town once had the luxury of being served by two branch lines, the first from Witham and the second from Woodham Ferrers, with terminus stations for each. Today, Maldon has no rail connection, while nearby Southminster, population 3,771, terminus of the electrified single-track

Crouch Valley line from Wickford, boasts an hourly service to Shenfield, which in the rush hour continues through to Liverpool Street.

It has been said that the Southminster branch not only survived but was upgraded because it was the closest to the nuclear power station at Bradwell-on-Sea. Nonetheless, the eradication of Maldon from the railway map will forever raise serious questions about the thinking behind the rationalisation of the national network, which had begun years before British Railways chairman Dr Beeching wielded his axe in 1963. Demands to restore at least one rail connection to Maldon will no doubt continue in perpetuity as the population grows.

The opening of the Eastern Counties Railway from London to Colchester in 1843 left towns and villages on the route wanting to maximise their slice of the benefits. In November 1845, a bill was deposited before Parliament for the building of a 12-mile railway linking Braintree with

Waiting to depart from Witham is the Maldon northern branch train headed by F5 2-4-2 tank No 8310 around 1930/1 (L.R. Peters collection)

Witham (on the main line) and Maldon, a port at the head of the river Blackwater which handled large tonnages of grain and potatoes. The Eastern Counties allowed the new line to cross the main line on the level, so as not to disrupt through running, with curves to link it to the Colchester route.

The Eastern Counties Railway purchased the shares from the proprietors and in 1847 the building contract was given to Thomas Jackson. The line opened on 2 October 1848, with intermediate stations at Bulford and Wickham Bishops. When the Bishop's Stortford to Dunmow and Braintree line was opened on 22 February 1869, the original Braintree station was relegated to a goods depot, and a new station was built.

There were other schemes to link Maldon to the railway network at the time, including one which would have run from Pitsea on the London, Tilbury & Southend Railway to Colchester via the port.

In the 1880s, the Great Eastern Railway set out to improve its access to Southend-on-Sea and opened a new route from Shenfield to Wickford on 19 November 1888, extending it to Southminster on 1 June 1889. When its main line reached Southend Victoria on 1 October 1889, a new branch between Woodham Ferrers (originally named Woodham Ferris) on the Southminster line and Maldon was opened.

A curve was installed at Wickford so that Southend trains could run straight through to Maldon without having to reverse, and another at Maldon itself, so that trains could run straight through on to the original branch if need be without having to reverse into the town's first station, which was renamed Maldon East, later becoming Maldon East & Heybridge. It has been conjectured that the curves were added at the request of the military, which saw the benefit for speeding up troop train movements in the event of any threat of invasion from the continent.

The southern Maldon branch, which was 8¾ miles in

Cold Norton station on the southern route to Maldon was an early casualty. (Lens of Sutton)

This postcard view describes Langford station as the only one in England having a stationmistress. (Lens of Sutton)

length, had intermediate stations at Cold Norton and Maldon West. The London & North Eastern Railway later opened halts at Baron's Lane and Stow St Mary. A short tunnel took the branch below Spital Road on the approach to Maldon East, crossing the river Chelmer by means of a large brick viaduct. A halt was later added to the northern branch at Langford & Ulting. The journey from Maldon to Witham took about 15 minutes. At Witham, Braintree branch locomotives had to run round their trains using the main line, while Maldon trains had their own loop.

While the Woodham Ferrers to Maldon service managed six trains daily before the First World War, passenger levels dropped in the twenties and thirties, and services were suspended on 10 September 1939 following the outbreak of war. The passenger trains on the southern branch never returned, apart from an occasional enthusiasts' excursion, but goods trains continued to use Maldon West until 31 January 1959.

The branch suffered the indignity of being used as a

A Maldon branch train headed by G4 0-4-4 tank No 8109 at Woodham Ferrers around 1930. (L.R. Peters collection)

storage siding for redundant steam stock following the electrification of the Liverpool Street to Shenfield line in 1949. When the old stock was taken to Stratford for scrapping in 1956, it had to come out via Maldon as the branch at the southern end had already been severed.

The stock had been neglected for so long that when a pair of J15 0-6-0 tender engines from Colchester came to move the carriages, branches of trees had grown through the windows, and metal door handles had been removed by scrap thieves, so that the doors had to be tied on with string.

Before the First World War, the Maldon to Witham branch had seven trains daily, and by 1937, this had been extended to ten a day, a figure restored in the late forties after wartime reductions. Locomotives on the Maldon to Witham line ranged from Class B12 4-6-0 tender engines to Great Eastern J15s, with F5 2-5-2 tank engines forming the mainstay of passenger services for many years.

Because of wooden trestle bridges on the line, only restrictions on axle loadings barred bigger engines. One day, one of the glamorous D16 class Claud Hamilton 4-6-0s went to Maldon by mistake, and was allowed back to Witham only after special permission was obtained from the district engineer.

Two-car diesel multiple units were introduced at the start of the 1956 timetable, and two years later German railbuses took over, cutting staffing costs at a stroke, with 18 trains each weekday from Witham to Maldon. The economies that were made were not enough to save either the Maldon to Witham or Braintree to Witham lines from being recommended for closure by Beeching.

Passenger services to Maldon ended on 7 September 1964, while freight continued until the branch closed to all traffic on 18 April 1966. It was the end for Maldon, but not for Braintree, where local residents under the banner of the Braintree & Witham Railway Committee launched a

A German-built railbus waits at Maldon East in the later days of the branch. (Bevan Price)

massive campaign to persuade more people to use the service.

In June 1963, the railbuses were replaced by diesel multiple units as passenger levels rose, and far from being closed, it was eventually decided to electrify the branch in the mid-seventies, the new services beginning on 3 October 1977. Like Southminster, it has an hourly service to Liverpool Street, and has also had a new station opened, Braintree Freeport, to serve an out-of-town retail park. Its latter-day success leaves Maldon residents wistfully thinking of what would have happened if their 'half' of the original line of 1848 had been afforded similar treatment.

The finest surviving relic of the Maldon branches is the ornate East station building, now listed and converted into offices, after a brief spell as a bar and restaurant. The sizeable brick-built four-road goods shed nearby which dated from 1848 was knocked down without prior notice

Magnificent Maldon East station survives in use as offices. (Author)

Maldon East's goods shed, which dated from 1848, served for many years in industrial use, but town residents were horrified to wake up over the Spring Bank Holiday weekend 2008 to find it had been knocked down without prior notice. (Author)

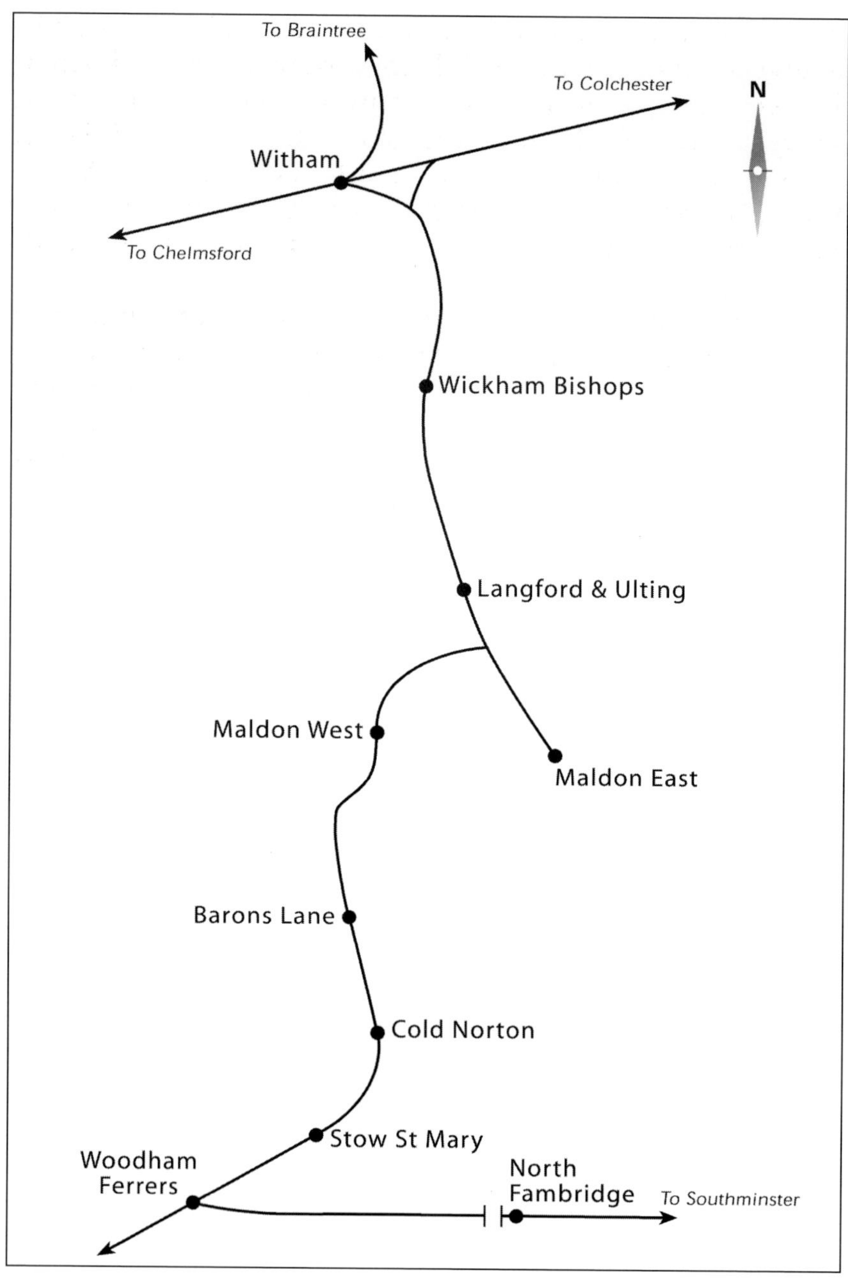
To Braintree
To Colchester
N
Witham
To Chelmsford
Wickham Bishops
Langford & Ulting
Maldon West
Maldon East
Barons Lane
Cold Norton
Stow St Mary
Woodham
Ferrers
North
Fambridge
To Southminster

over the Spring Bank Holiday weekend in 2008, leading to an investigation by the local district council. The trackbed of the old railway from here is now covered by the town bypass, with the Maldon West site at the other end. Here, the old yard is now an industrial estate with one old brick-built railway shed remaining. North of the town, the platform at Langford & Ulting Halt survives beneath undergrowth.

The route of both lines can still be followed, with the northern one forming the Blackwater Rail Trail footpath, managed as a linear country park by Essex County Council, although several bridges have been infilled. The southern section is in the possession of several private owners, and each year nature reclaims still more.

7
To the Seaside

The Kelvedon & Tollesbury Light Railway
(The Crab and Winkle line)
The Brightlingsea branch
Walton-on-the-Naze pier railway
The Jaywick Sands Miniature Railway
Other lost miniature railways
Mangapps Railway Museum

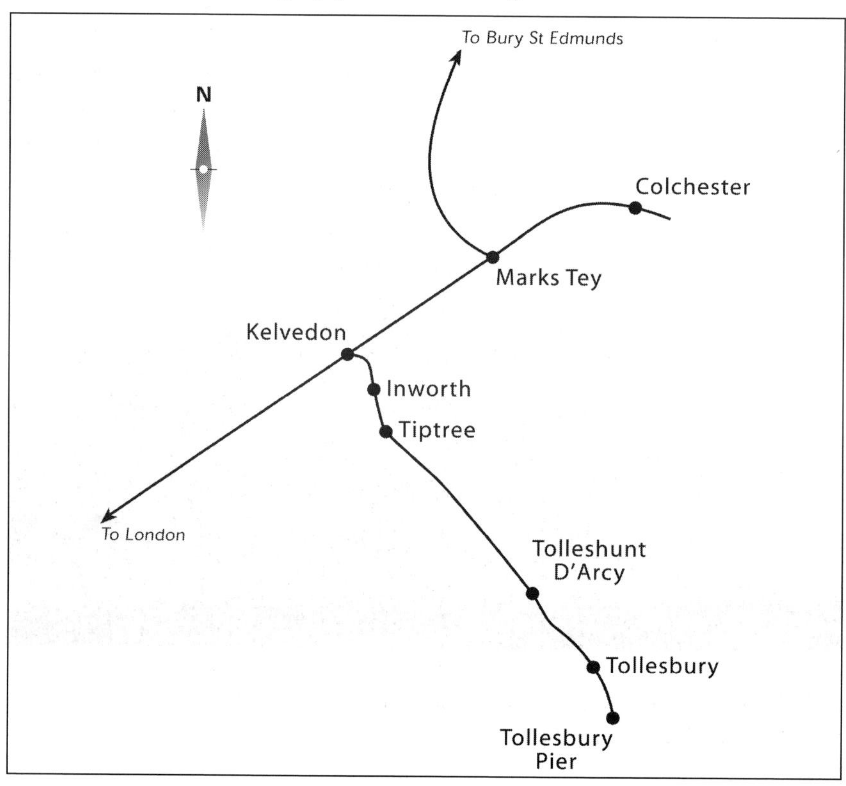

The Kelvedon & Tollesbury Light Railway (the Crab and Winkle Line)

The Kelvedon & Tollesbury Light Railway may well have been the most delightful of the Essex lines that are no longer with us, if only for its eccentric assortment of rolling stock, let alone the grandiose aims of its promoters. The Light Railways Act of 1896, which was intended to reduce hardship in remote and poor rural areas, and was passed just before the advent of the motor car, spawned a plethora of lines built very much on the cheap, acquiring second-hand stock and carriages from various sources, and using old coach bodies to double up as station waiting rooms.

In many ways, the light railways of the time were the predecessors of today's preserved or heritage railways, where locomotives and carriages long since discarded by the national network were given a second lease of life in a localised and often Ruritanian setting where they were limited to a maximum of 25 mph.

J67 0-6-0 No 7169 outside Kelvedon shed on 27 March 1957. (Gresley Society/Jack Dulieu collection)

A unique survivor: Kelvedon & Tollesbury coach No 8 being restored for use on the North Norfolk Railway. (North Norfolk Railway)

Plans for a line from Kelvedon to Tollesbury were duly deposited with the Light Railway Commissioners on 27 May 1897, and the Light Railway Order was granted on 29 January 1901. However, building work did not begin until early in 1903, and the opening was delayed by heavy rain from summer 1904 until 1 October that year.

The line ran from the Great Eastern Railway main line from London to Colchester at Kelvedon with intermediate stations at Feering, Inworth, Tiptree, Tolleshunt Knights and Tolleshunt D'Arcy, and there was a short extension from Tollesbury to Tollesbury Pier which opened in May 1907. Tollesbury is still a remote place today, and many visitors who come to enjoy walks along the coast are surprised to learn that not only was it once served by a railway, but had two stations into the bargain.

Tiptree is famous for its jam making. One of the railway's promoters was Arthur C. Wilkin whose Britannia Fruit Preserving Company at Tiptree, makers of Wilkins Jam, was

Tolleshunt D'Arcy, an intermediate station between Tiptree and Tollesbury, as seen in 1950. (GERS/Real Photographs)

eager to benefit most from cheaper freight transport, and he gave much land for the building of the line free of charge.

However, the line's backers wanted much more – and hoped to see tiny Tollesbury developed as a fully-fledged continental port! The wooden pier at Tollesbury was meant to be a landing place for ship passengers, but this aspect of the line never took off. Neither did Tollesbury Pier as a centre for yachting on the river Blackwater, as had been hoped. The estuary was muddy, and could not compete as a tourist magnet with the sandy beaches at Clacton-on-Sea and Walton-on-the Naze, which were also served by rail.

The First World War finally put an end to any lingering dreams of building a major port, and the pier extension was closed to passengers on 18 July 1921, but remained in use for goods. Locally-caught shrimps and other seafood were the primary goods for freight traffic, hence its nickname – the Crab and Winkle line.

The Great Eastern Railway ran the line from the start. Traffic was handled by the company's tank engines, normally Class J67 0-6-0s. The first locomotive to work on the line was GER 0-6-2 tank engine No 25, which dated from 1877 and which was scrapped as early as 1905.

As tickets were always issued on the trains to save paying for station staff, tram-type carriages were needed, and the GER converted eight six-wheelers to corridor stock with vestibule connections and steps for boarding, as the station platforms were so low. A gangway was cut through the middle of each coach so that the guard collected fares after walking through the train to take orders and then returning to his van to make out the tickets, which were printed at the GER's Stratford works.

The pier, which extended 1,770 ft into the river Blackwater, had a new lease of life during the Second World War, when it was co-opted into the local coastal defence system, and four War Department locomotives complete with mobile guns were stationed there.

In 1928, when passenger services ended on the equally-quaint Wisbech & Upwell Tramway in Cambridgeshire, two of its coaches, numbers 7 and 8, which dated from 1884, were transferred to the Tollesbury line. Very unusual for 20th-century Britain, they had end platforms with elaborate wrought-iron railings. The pair were among the last gas-lit coaches to run on British Railways.

The launch of a bus service from Tollesbury to Kelvedon and Witham in the 1920s hit the line's passenger levels hard, but services lingered on until 5 May 1951. Most of the line beyond the Tudwick Road fruit collection sidings east of Tiptree was closed completely on 29 October that year. Apart from the jam factory, a printing works, a brewery and a coal merchant used the remainder of the line until freight services, largely handled by Great Eastern Railway J15 0-6-0 tender engines, were withdrawn on 1 October 1962. Very little now remains on the ground to show that a railway ever existed. However, the story of the line did not end there. The two Wisbech & Upwell carriages were stored at the Stratford depot in East London after the Tollesbury line closed. Coach No 8 was used in the Ealing comedy *The Titfield Thunderbolt*,

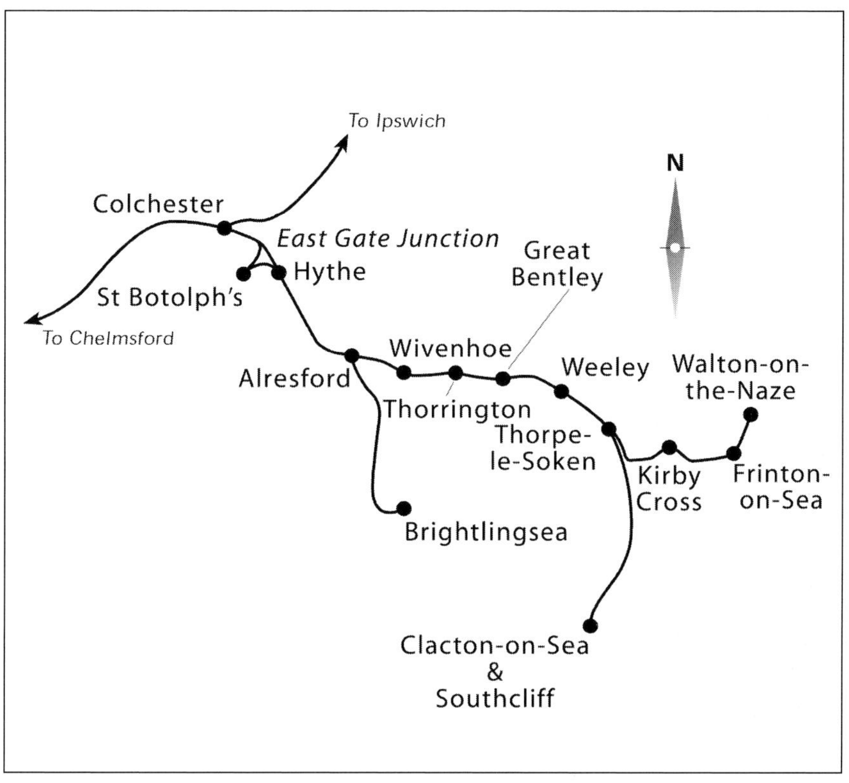

a 1953 hit movie starring Stanley Holloway which told the story of villagers trying to save their branch line from closure.

Indeed, the film makers had considered using the Tollesbury branch for filming, only to decide in favour of Limpley Stoke near Bath instead. When the filming was over, No 8 was returned to Stratford with the aim of preserving it, but it ended up being scrapped in 1954. No 7 was also sold for scrap, but was used as an onion store before the body was acquired by the Rutland Railway Museum in 1982.

In 2002, the coach was transferred to the Midland & Great Northern Joint Railway Society which has restored it for use on the North Norfolk Railway at Sheringham, with the aim of running recreated Wisbech & Upwell trains.

So at least a little piece of the Tollesbury branch survives, albeit on the other side of East Anglia, and can be enjoyed by future generations who might like to experience a taste of the transport of yesteryear from this lonely part of the eastern Essex coast.

The Brightlingsea branch

The area between the estuaries of the rivers Stour and Colne in north-east Essex is historically known as the Tendring Hundred. It received its first railway incursion when a goods branch was built by the Colchester, Stour Valley & Halstead Railway from Colchester to the Hythe, a busy port on the Colne, with the terminus station opening in 1847.

The Tendring Hundred Railway built a line from Hythe to Wivenhoe, opening it in 1863, and extended it in 1866 by a single track line from East Gate and Hythe junctions to a small central Colchester station at St Botolph's in 1866.

That year, the line extended eastwards to Weeley, and it reached Walton-on-the-Naze in 1867, and Clacton-on-Sea in 1882, with spectacular results for the development of the holiday trade in both resorts, especially the latter. A bill for the Wivenhoe & Brightlingsea Railway was deposited in Parliament in November 1860, but legal disputes about costs led to it not being opened until 18 April 1866.

There were no intermediate stations on the five-mile line, which largely hugged the northern shore of the Colne estuary before crossing marshland on an embankment and Alresford Creek over a swing bridge and entering Brightlingsea Town. It was worked by the Great Eastern Railway in return for 40 per cent of receipts. The Great Eastern finally bought the line in 1891. A three-mile extension of the line to St Osyth had been planned, but the costs proved too daunting for investors, with steep gradients involved. Many branch trains operated out of St Botolph's station, and it took about 12 minutes to make the journey from Wivenhoe.

The original Brightlingsea station was burned down on New Year's Eve 1901, with local people who detested its draughtiness celebrating its passing by singing *Auld Lang Syne* nearby. The goods station served the nearby gas works, boat slipways and fish-landing causeway. Because Brightlingsea had a thriving Pyfleet oyster industry, at least one fish van was coupled to almost every outgoing passenger train. Shipbuilding also provided a major source of freight. The signal box and signals were decommissioned as early as 1922, being replaced by basic ground frames and leaving the branch to be worked on the one-engine-in-steam principle.

In the 1930s, which were probably the heyday of passenger traffic, there were ten midweek return trips, another two on Saturdays and seven on Sundays, and it was possible to make a return journey from London in about one and three-quarter hours. This rose to 12 or 13 trains each way by the late forties. Cheap day fares on Bank Holidays saw heavy loadings, underlining the value of the short branch for trippers.

Locomotive power on the line varied from Great Eastern 2-4-2 tank engines from classes F3, F4, F5 and F7 and North Eastern Railway G5 class 0-4-4 tanks, to the workaday J15 0-6-0 tender engines, which became the mainstay of traffic from 1939. However, occasional visits by the more glamorous D16 Claud Hamilton 4-6-0 tender engines were made.

Three miles of the track were washed away during the floods of January 1953, with British Railways causing uproar by proposing to close the branch to save the expense of

The 'new' Brightlingsea station, which replaced the draughty original which burned down, as seen from the road. (Lens of Sutton)

J15 0-6-0 No 65432 takes on water at Brightlingsea in the 1950s before coupling back up to its train. (Pyfleet Pictures)

repair work. However, the line was reinstated, and services resumed on 7 December that year, the first train leaving Brightlingsea behind J15 No 65432 to the sound of blasts from the whistle and exploding railway detonators.

Diesel multiple units replaced steam trains on the line in the mid-fifties, when around 3,000 people still rode on the branch in winter and 5,000 in summer. However, Dr Beeching's report in 1963 claimed that it would need 17,000 passengers a week to make the line viable, and so his axe fell. The last trains ran on 14 June 1964.

Brightlingsea station has long since been demolished, a caravan site now taking its place, with a community centre built on the exact spot, but the remains of the embankment over the marshes, which continues to serve as a defence against flooding, and the pillars for the swing bridge can still be seen. The Station Tavern in Station Road is still open for business.

The town, the only Cinque Port in Essex, is now mainly a dormitory settlement for Colchester, and a popular retirement destination. Even if it did not pay its way, it could

British Railways' Eastern Region was the first to eliminate steam, but even the savings made by introducing diesel services could not save lines like the Brightlingsea branch. (Bevan Price)

be argued that the branch provided a valuable community service, and could still do so today, had it survived.

Walton-on-the-Naze pier railway

The world's longest seaside pier is to be found at Southend-on-Sea. Extended to 7,080 ft in 1897, it is so long that it needs a railway of its own to transport visitors from one end to the other. Essex also has the country's third longest pier, at Walton-on-the-Naze, and it too had a railway of its own.

The original Walton pier was the fourth in Britain to be built when it opened in 1830. The 300 ft-long wooden jetty was used solely for the landing of goods and passengers on the 'Belle' steamers running between London and Great Yarmouth. Sixty years later it was badly damaged in a storm, but by then the British seaside resort and its trademark pier had taken off big time. The owner, the

A view of Walton Pier showing the original tramway and its electric cars. (Putmans Photographic archive)

A 1950s 'Hi De Hi'-type train hauled by locomotive Dreadnought *runs to the end of Walton Pier. (Putmans Photographic archive)*

Walton-on-the-Naze Hotel and Pier Company, opened a new 800 ft pier in 1895, with successive extensions due to shoreline changes extending it to 2,600 ft.

To take passengers and their luggage to the pierhead as efficiently as possible, a 3 ft 6 in single-track electric tramway was laid on the pier deck. There were three 'toastrack' carriages, one providing the traction and the other two trailer cars. This tramway lasted until 1935 when it was replaced by a battery-powered carriage.

Pleasure steamers were the pier's main trade until the Second World War, after which, like its counterparts elsewhere, it refocused on children's amusements.

The pier was ravaged by a fire in 1942 which damaged the battery carriage. Contractors repairing wartime damage laid a 2 ft gauge track on the decking to bring raw materials in, and when they left, the line was left in place to be used as a new pleasure line. Traction was provided by an 0-4-0 diesel locomotive, *Dreadnought*, which like many amusement park railway locomotives, had been built to resemble a steam engine, in 1948.

The railway stopped running in 1978 after the pier was badly damaged in a storm and the tracks were lifted. *Dreadnought*, built by Baguley of Burton-on-Trent, was delivered new to Wilson's Pleasure Railway at Allhallows-on-Sea in Kent in 1939. After the pier line closed, *Dreadnought* was sold to the Camelot Theme Park at Charnock Richard in Lancashire, and was renamed *The Lady Guinevere*. It is now based at the Amerton Railway, an enthusiast line at Stowe-by-Chartley near Stafford, where it re-entered service in 2000 after being rebuilt to its original condition.

The Jaywick Sands Miniature Railway

On 31 July 1936, an 18 in gauge miniature railway was opened in the resort of Jaywick near Clacton-on-Sea. The village had originally been intended as a holiday resort for Londoners, but expanded when more and more people decided to stay.

The pleasure-beach line was owned by the Miniature Railway & Specialist Engineering Company and was formally opened by Mr C.H. Newton, the divisional general manager of the Southern area of the London & North Eastern Railway. The little railway was a mile long and ran from Jaywick Sands along a dyke to the Tudor Village at Clacton and a terminus at Crossways. One unusual feature was a 60 ft tunnel which had been driven through an Iron Age long barrow.

The sole steam locomotive was a miniature Great Northern Railway, Stirling single 4-2-2 No 1, a model of which is now in the National Railway Museum at York. The model was built at the Regent Street Polytechnic from a set

A contemporary postcard showing the short-lived Jaywick Sands Railway. (Nigel Bowdidge collection)

of parts supplied by W.G. Bagnall of Stafford. It was sold to the Fairbourne Railway near Barmouth in 1926, and a decade later moved to Jaywick, where it was named *Century*.

Because of problems with the steam locomotive due to water quality, the line later acquired a model of a Sentinel geared-drive vertical-boiler locomotive. The line had three luxurious eight-seater bogie carriages illuminated by electric light. Operations ceased when war broke out in September 1939, never to be resumed. The steam locomotive is now a static exhibit at the World of Country Life museum at Sandy Bay near Exmouth.

The Sentinel locomotive and stock were sold to the New Brighton Miniature Railway, and the coaches found their way to Cumbria's Ravenglass & Eskdale Railway in 1965 and were regauged to 15 in. Two of the carriages survive in an unrestored condition at the Windmill Farm Railway at Burscough in Lancashire.

Other lost miniature railways

When it was regarded as a mainstream holiday resort, Southend-on-Sea was home to a series of miniature railways. There was a 200-yard-long 15 in gauge line at the Kursaal (a German name meaning 'cure hall' or 'spa'). This was a listed building, built around 1920, that was once one of the resort's main attractions. The line was operated by a Hershall-Spillman 4-4-0 locomotive with four Bassett-Lowke four-wheeled open coaches.

This line was acquired by Harold and Nigel Parkinson, operators of a miniature line at Great Yarmouth, in 1930, and was extended to a quarter of a mile with new stations added at Lakeside and Central, which had an overall roof.

Two more locomotives arrived, Bassett-Lowke Little Giant class 4-4-0 *George the Fifth* from Skegness, and Bassett-Lowke Class 30 4-4-2 locomotive *Synolda* which had been built for the Sand Hutton Light Railway in Yorkshire.

The railway closed in 1938, and the stock was sold to a buyer from Bishop Auckland in County Durham. *George the Fifth* ended up at the now-closed Steamtown museum at Carnforth in Lancashire and in 2000 was exported to the United States after being sold at auction, while *Synolda* is now at the Ravenglass & Eskdale Railway.

After the Second World War, another railway was laid at the Kursall. This 10¼ in gauge line used an American-style Curwen 4-4-2 as motive power. The floods of 1953 which devastated much of the east coast leaving death and mass destruction in their wake brought a swift end to this railway, which was left buried under piles of sand.

A third railway was briefly operated on Southend's seafront, a quarter-mile-long 15 in gauge concern on which a Bassett-Lowke Little Giant class 4-4-2 ran. Finally, a 10¼ in gauge line was laid near the Marine Parade boating lake for a distance of around a quarter of a mile, its first motive

Bassett-Lowke locomotive Synolda *once ran on a miniature railway at Southend-on-Sea. (Ravenglass & Eskdale Railway)*

power being a model of a LNER V2 class 2-6-2 built at Sheringham in Norfolk. The line closed in 1986.

A 7¼ in gauge miniature railway which operated at North Benfleet – and was aptly titled the North Benfleet Miniature Railway – was later acquired for use at the Barleylands Railway, which opened in 1989 at Barleylands Visitor Centre, Billericay and which now has six steam engines.

There was also a mile-long 7¼ in gauge line at Coalhouse Fort in East Tilbury, which had a seven-coach model of the short-lived British Rail Advanced Passenger Train and a miniature version of a six-coach High Speed Train set. The line closed in 1984.

Mangapps Railway Museum

Do old Essex railways ever really die – or do they end up at Mangapps Railway Museum, a short hop from the coast near Burnham-on-Crouch?

The museum at Mangapps Farm, with its own running line, has been progressively built up by farmer and lifelong enthusiast John Jolly and his wife June since the 1980s. Today, the museum boasts one of the biggest collections of railway relics in Britain, including many items from the lost lines contained in this book. Visitors will quickly see an old blue enamel nameboard from Silvertown station on the North Woolwich line, another, Audley End for Saffron

A recreation of a wonderful Essex country scene of the mid-fifties, with J15 No 65462 waiting to pick up goods while a farmer chats to the local bobby, staged at Mangapps Railway Museum. (Geoff Silcock)

Relics of Essex stations and railway furniture of yesteryear inside Mangapps Railway Museum. (Author)

Walden, from the western end of the Saffron Walden branch, and a platform seat labelled Maldon (East) & Heybridge.

Its comprehensive railway signalling equipment collection is the biggest of its kind on public display in Britain and includes a working lever frame connected to a set of signals, which visitors can try for themselves.

However, the biggest attraction is the ¾ mile-long operational standard gauge line. Mangapps Farm was never situated on a railway, or connected to one, and John has built everything on a virgin green field site. Both steam and diesel trains are run. Indeed, the sight of the museum's diesel multiple unit in the station at Mangapps is so evocative of the final years of many of the rural Essex routes which were closed.

One of the latest additions to the complex is a restored Great Central Railway coach which has been turned into luxury accommodation and can be booked for short breaks.

One of the big advantages of Mangapps in terms of railway preservation is that the museum is in single ownership, and is run as ancillary to the farm. It answers only to John and June, and unlike most other heritage railway venues in the country, they do not have to justify their reasons for bringing items of stock to the spacious site. Therefore we see London Underground tube cars and electric multiple units preserved: they would never be able to run on a preserved railway by themselves because of the lack of a live rail, yet if the railway preservation movement

This is so typical of many a lost Essex branch line in its final years, when diesel multiple units replaced steam in a vain attempt to convince people that sufficient savings could be made. However, this is the terminus station at Mangapps Railway Museum, which has been created on a green field site to remember what was once commonplace in the county. (Author)

is serious about preserving historical items for the benefit of future generations, examples of these surely deserve to be saved.

Similarly, a modern bogie petrol-tank wagon which served an Essex refinery has been saved: it would never fit in with the ambience of most preserved lines, but if it had not been found a home and had been scrapped, the type would have become extinct.

Through having many items on display with a London and Essex connection, Mangapps is making a significant contribution to the region's transport heritage, complementing similar work being done at the Colne Valley Railway and East Anglian Railway Museum, and providing an essential bolthole for items which might so easily be lost, along with the lines they once served.

8
Waltham Abbey Royal Gunpowder Mills

An explosive tale

The marshalling yard at the new Gunpowder Mills railway system, with typical Ministry of Defence narrow gauge vans lined up.

The Royal Gunpowder Mills at Waltham Abbey are now unique in Britain. One of three gunpowder mill sites in the British Isles, the others being at Ballincollig and Faversham, it is the only one that is still intact. Not only that, but its once-extensive internal railway system is being revived.

The site was in use for more than three centuries and, from the 1850s onwards, was concerned with the development of new nitro-based explosives and propellants, which superseded gunpowder production. The superior production methods earned Waltham Abbey a global reputation and made a major contribution to the rise of the United Kingdom as a world power.

The history of the mills at Waltham Abbey, which was founded around 1030, dates back to the time when the medieval monks established a fulling mill for cloth production. Early in the 17th century, the mill was adapted to produce vegetable oils. During the Second Dutch War (1665-67), the oil mill was converted for gunpowder production by Ralph Hudson, using saltpetre made in Bedfordshire and Hertfordshire as the basic ingredient. At the end of the 17th century, Hudson sold the concern to William Walton, leading to a rapid expansion of gunpowder production. Indeed, the mills were one of the first examples of an industrialised factory system. In October 1878, the Government bought the mills from John Walton at the instigation of Major, later Lieutenant General, Sir William Congreve, Deputy Controller of the Royal Laboratory at Woolwich, who applied further significant developments in technology.

The volume and quality of production were stepped up in response to the threats from across the Channel during the French Revolution and the Napoleonic Wars. Further advances in gunpowder production and chemical engineering were again made during the Crimean War and the Boer War, while the need for explosives in civil engineering of the 19th century such as mining, quarrying, tunnelling and the building of railways opened up fresh markets for the output.

Under Sir Frederick Abel, guncotton and cordite were developed at Waltham Abbey, which had become a world leader in terms of science and technology.

The site featured in the H.G. Wells science-fiction classic *The War of the Worlds*, when, following rumours of Martians landing at Epping, Waltham Abbey Powder Mills are destroyed in a fruitless attempt to blow up one of the invaders.

The First World War saw staff numbers doubled to around 6,230 to cope with demand, and afterwards development work was carried out on TNT and a new explosive, RDX, of which the site was the sole manufacturer for the first two years of the Second World War.

That conflict saw new Royal Ordnance factories established throughout the country, and while Waltham Abbey staff played a key role in setting them up and training staff, the Royal Gunpowder Mills finally closed in 1943.

It reopened as the Explosives Research and Development Establishment, a research centre, in 1945, and in 1977 became the Propellants, Explosives and Rocket Motor Establishment, taking the technology into the space age with the development of rocket propellants and motors, as well as specialised applications such as cartridges for firing aircraft ejector seats.

In 1984, the southern part of the site was transferred to Royal Ordnance plc, while the north side became part of the Ministry of Defence Royal Armament Research Development Establishment. The centre finally closed in 1991. With financial help from the Heritage Lottery Fund, most of the north site and its many historical buildings was saved for the nation, and a heritage visitor centre was established at the centre of what are now 165 acres of parkland following decontamination.

It was inevitable that such a sprawling site would have needed transport to bring in raw materials and to move finished products. The surviving parts of an extensive canal system and special barges built for carrying explosives can be seen. The site also had an internal railway network, dating back to the Crimean War, when new steam-powered mills were built from 1856 to help with the vastly-increased demand.

The first railway on the site – a 2 ft 3 in gauge line – connected the charcoal mill and gunpowder-mixing house

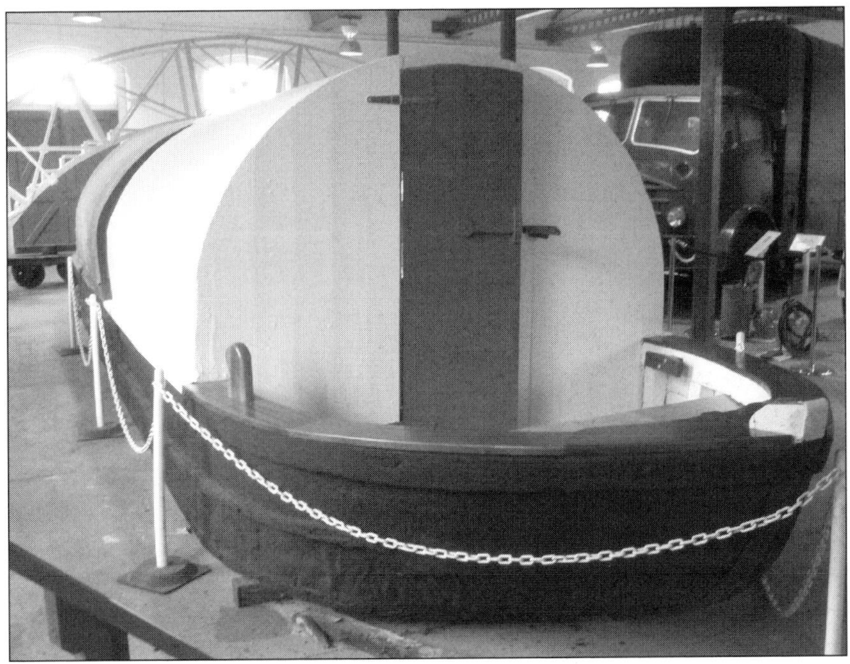

One of the reinforced steel barges which once carried explosives around Waltham Abbey. The munitions works had a canal system as well as a railway. (Author)

to the mills on the south side of Queen's Mead and the main canal to the east. The system used wooden rails faced with iron on the top and inner surfaces, and the track mainly ran on raised wooden platforms level with the floors of the mills. Wagons were pushed by hand.

One of the specialist wagons used on the internal system which has now been restored. (Author)

In 1862, the London & North Western Railway introduced an 18 in gauge system at its massive Crewe Works. The advantages of this very narrow gauge, which is far better known for its use in pleasure park and seaside miniature railways, was that materials and components could be moved easily and safely into each building, as tight track curves were possible.

The government immediately saw the advantage of 18 in gauge internal systems and introduced them at key sites like Woolwich Arsenal and Chatham Dockyard. The internal lines at Waltham Abbey were converted to 18 in gauge by 1897, and as the site expanded, so did its railway network. All-wooden rails were used in the cordite factory to avoid any risk of sparks from steel wheels running on steel rails in an explosive environment, and some of these can still be seen on the site today.

The First World War saw more miles added to the railway system, with a line 3½-miles long capable of carrying locomotives built to connect the mills on the north side of Highbridge Street to those on the south. In turn, this linked to the standard gauge branch from the Liverpool Street to Cambridge main line serving Enfield Royal Small Arms Factory and the coal wharf serving the mills on the bank of the river Lee, where exchange sidings between the two gauges were installed. Three swing bridges were built to allow for barges beneath the line, and a tunnel was built beneath Highbridge Street.

Because of the threat of explosions caused by sparks, steam locomotives were not used on the line. At the start, four Ruston Proctor paraffin-powered locomotives were bought in 1917, capable of hauling up to nine loaded bogie wagons at speeds of up to 6 mph. They were joined, and eventually replaced, by a fleet of small battery-powered electric locomotives.

The railway had a series of bespoke wagons for various

specialist purposes, such as carrying guncotton and cordite as well as baskets of laundry. Because of the secrecy which surrounded the operation of the site, it has not been established whether it ever carried passengers.

The railway system closed in 1954, and houses in Beaulieu Drive have been built on the site of the engine shed and main sidings. With the establishment of the visitor centre at Royal Gunpowder Mills, plans were drawn up by volunteer supporters to lay a new 18 in gauge railway – but this time round, because there are no explosives anywhere on the site, steam engines could be used.

Avonside 0-4-0 side tank Woolwich, *built in 1916, now forms part of the 'new' locomotive fleet at the gunpowder mills. (Author)*

Carnegie, a bogie Hunslet diesel dating from 1954, has joined the modern-day Waltham Abbey fleet. (Author)

In 2000, the revivalists bought rolling stock from the Bicton Woodlands Railway at Bicton Gardens near Budleigh Salterton in south-east Devon, most of which had in turn been acquired from Woolwich Arsenal. While the stock never ran at the mills, it was built to similar War Department designs. For instance, the coach bodies are on frames and bogies identical to those used at Waltham Abbey in 1917 for large cordite wagons. The mills' 'new' fleet of locomotives includes Avonside 0-4-0 tank engine *Woolwich*, built in Bristol in 1916, and the only survivor of 16 from the arsenal, and the unique bogie diesel locomotive *Carnegie*, which was built by Hunslet of Leeds in 1954, also for Woolwich.

The former military depot rolling stock that has been amassed at Waltham Abbey on the relaid internal rail system. (Author)

In 2003, the closure of the Royal Ordnance Factory at Bishopton near Paisley, to where most of Waltham Abbey's production had been switched by 1943, led to a large quantity of 2 ft 6 in gauge stock and track components being donated to the mills and a line is being developed on the western side of the Waltham Abbey site, and with an 18 in gauge line to the east. It is hoped to develop a transfer point where visitors can switch from one line to the other.

Original tramway plates rescued by archaeologists from Woolwich Arsenal, including the only surviving complete wagon turntable, have also been moved to the site.

The Royal Gunpowder Mills has been designated as an 'anchor point' on the European Route of Industrial Heritage, an international network of the most important industrial heritage sites covering 29 countries.

Conclusion

Despite being monopolised by two companies, the Great Eastern Railway and to a smaller extent the London Tilbury & Southend Railway, Essex has a rich, varied and truly fascinating railway history.

In terms of lines forced out of existence by competition from road traffic, Essex has probably fared better than most other English counties, with relatively few closures. Occasionally there are calls for some of them, like one of the two lines that once served Maldon, or the route from Epping to Ongar, now an embryonic heritage railway, to be reopened, in the face of rising fuel costs and worsening congestion, plus the never-satisfied need to build more houses on the fringes of the capital.

The railway map of Essex may have retreated somewhat in the second half of the 20th century, but it advanced again with the building of a short branch to serve a new station at Stansted Airport in 1991.

The second decade of the 21st century will see the closed North Woolwich branch converted into three separate rail systems – an extension to a London Underground line, a part of the Docklands Light Railway and a section of the planned new Crossrail scheme for London, and so will survive, albeit in a dissected and very altered state.

Like their counterparts elsewhere, Essex folk felt passionately about losing rail services, and scored rare victories when the lines to Braintree and Sudbury were saved, and they clearly will not hesitate to take up the protest banners again. In 2006, residents of genteel Frinton-on-Sea, served by the Walton-on-the-Naze branch, and often labelled Britain's most conservative town, mounted a vociferous campaign to stop Network Rail replacing its famous traditional wooden level-crossing gates with a modern automatic barrier. The gates feature prominently in the logo of Frinton and Walton Town Council and are seen as the entrance to the town. Outraged Frinton deputy mayor Terry Allen proclaimed: 'Paris has its Eiffel Tower, London has Tower Bridge and in Frinton, we have the gates.'

It has even been claimed that the gates are an essential crime-fighting tool, because when a burglary takes place, the police telephone the crossing keeper and tell him to keep them shut, preventing the culprits leaving the town by car. Councillors have said that they have done their job safely for over a century, so why replace them? However, Network Rail announced that it was due to start work on replacing

The level-crossing gates which provide a 'drawbridge' into Frinton-on-Sea. (Author)

the gates on 26 August 2008, despite a request from Lord Hanningfield, the leader of Essex County Council, for more consultations with local people to take place. Local railway heritage can be a highly emotive subject, and there are many who will fight to keep it intact, and do their utmost to prevent more parts of the system, no matter how small, from going the way of the lines in Essex that have already been lost.

Index